Live from death row

Live from death row

Mumia Abu-Jamal

Introduction by John Edgar Wideman

Addison-Wesley Publishing Company
Reading, Massachusetts Menlo Park, California New York
Don Mills, Ontario Wokingham, England Amsterdam
Bonn Sydney Singapore Tokyo Madrid San Juan Paris
Seoul Milan Mexico City Taipei

"Teetering on the Brink Between Life and Death" reprinted with permission from the *Yale Law Journal*.

"B-Block Days and Nightmares" reprinted with permission from *The Nation*.

"On Death Row: Fade to Black" from *A Saga of Shame: Racial Discrimination and the Death Penalty* reprinted with permission from Equal Justice/USA.

Library of Congress Cataloging-in-Publication Data
Abu-Jamal, Mumia.
    Live from death row / Mumia Abu-Jamal.
      p.   cm.
    ISBN 0-201-48319-X
    1. Death row—United States.   2. Criminal justice,
Administration of—United States.   3. Race discrimination—
United States.   4. Afro-Americans—Legal status, laws, etc.
5. Abu-Jamal, Mumia.   6. Death row inmates—United States—
Biography.   I. Title.
HV8699.U5A65   1995
364.6'6'092—dc20   94-45952
                                           CIP

Jacket design by Jean Seal
Text design by Janis Owens
Set in 11-point Janson by Pagesetters, Inc., Brattleboro, VT

4 5 6 7 8 9-DOH-9998979695
Fourth printing, August 1995

To Edith L. and William H., two Southern souls, one dimpled, high cheekboned, the color and aroma of sweet potatoes, the other short, muscular, coffee-colored (sans cream), embodiment of gruff love, auraed by cigar smoke (Phillies), who both joined the Great Migration North in search of that fabled land of Equality, Opportunity, and Freedom for all.

'Up Nawth'—the Northern tier of a Mason-Dixon line that marked the U.S.–Canadian border for some African-Americans—was a cold and harsh land that shattered some illusions, only to breed others.

For the children it was home.

For them it was the Promised Land.

To them, who scuffed and scraped to bring their brood a new and better world.

To their world, which might have been.

Contents

Contents

part two   **Crime and punishment**

part three   **Musings, memories, and prophecies**

Acknowledgments

Kudos supreme to J.E.W.—masterful in his introduction. Wow! Like Pharaoh Sanders with a pen instead of a sax!

The late, revered Dr. Huey P. Newton, in his book *Revolutionary Suicide*,* once wrote of his admiration for the African axiom "I am we," the natural notion that the tribe and the individual are one. In the spirit of that ancient wisdom I wish to acknowledge my debt to the many members of the Eternal Tribe; to the Nameless Ones who braved hell's storms to make that wretched Middle Passage, from West Africa to the American southlands; to the Blessed Reverend Nat Turner, who danced to Heaven's Horn; to Gabriel Prosser—among those who blew it;

---

* Huey P. Newton, *Revolutionary Suicide*. New York: Harcourt Brace & Jovanovich, 1973.

to Shaka and those who held the line at Island-whana.

To the spiritual sons and daughters of *John Africa* and the martyrs of the May 13th massacre; to Pam, Bert, Ria, Mona, Theresa, Mo, Mary, Mella Swella and Franco—to Puga, Rhonda, Jay, Tiffany, Malachide, Boosh—all the Seeds of Wisdom, to Rose and Pixie—to Bev; to all who wear the name Africa; to alla dem; to Ras Marley—and to all others who have sung for Babylon's fall; to Elder Curtis Mayfield, whose sweet rebel songs echoed across America, & helped many a Panther pass the day, singing, "We're a winner, and never let anybody say that y'all can't make it, 'cuz them people's mind is in yo' way . . ."; to rads and rebels worldwide, to Amerika Gegeninformationspresse (AGIPA), Partisan Defense Committee (PDC), New Afrikan Network in Support of Political Prisoners and Prisoners of War (NANPPOW), Assata, NAACP Legal Defense and Education Fund, Demba Diop, Heike, Jürgen, Regine and Marleentja, Susanne, and the German crew, the nameless ones who did the indispensable work that makes a movement grow and touch others—to Yatamah, Cory, The three Lindas (two Thurstons and one Ragin), William Goldsby, Abdul Jon, Bobby B., John and Jenny Black (two from the same fire), Fred Horstmann, Shep, Yuri and Jamila; to the good bloods and folks toiling still in the bowels of Babylon, to Dr. Mutulu Shakur, Sundiata Acoli, geronimo ji jaga (Pratt), Jihaad, Mzilikazi; to PPS and the Black Cultural work-shop's crew—Kojo, Emory Ghana, Leonard Peltier—to Ruchell Magee, sole survivor of the Marin County Courthouse massacre, acquitted by the jury but damned by the state, in California dungeons since 1971 (and in other California gulags for at least twenty years before that).

To Ray Luc Lavasseur, Larry Giddings, to Stephen Luther Evans, a jailhouse lawyer ex-traordinaire who opened the door for countless dudes, but who had death slam the door before he could take that long walk to freedom. To the lawyers outside who struggle to help me join them; to Leonard I. Weinglass, Esq.; Steven Hawkins, NAACP Legal Defense and Edu-cation Fund, Dan Williams; to Rachel "The Reminder" Wolkenstein; and Jonathan Piper, associate counsel; to Adjoa Aiyetoro National Conference of Black Lawyers (NCBL), Jacqué Reardon, and Ashanti Chimurenga, Lawyas of the New Age. TO ALL BEHIND BABYLON'S WALLS, to Del, China, Phil, Neen, Janet, Ed, Mike, Deb, and Chuck—soldiers and ministers of *John Africa's Revolution* who are doing a century in Pennsylvania's hellholes for refusing to betray their faith in the teaching, despite their innocence; who are prisoners of a political order bent on their destruction on August 8, 1978, May 13, 1985, and even this very day.

To Whoopi!, Danny Glover; the dynamic duo of Ossie Davis and Ruby Dee; artists who have evoked imagery of a progressive ethos and who have dared to breach the barriers between art and life, like Ed Asner and Mike Farrell. To Alhaji Bai Konte; to Griots known and unknown, Del Jones, Linn Washington, Father Paul Washington, Cody Anderson, Kamau, Jah Free I, Terry Bisson, Doc (aka Dr. Alan Berkman ex–political prisoner who did time with me in Holmesburg Dungeon), Judy Douglass, Jo Nina Ambron, Askia Muhammed; to former fellow Panther turned Griot-Kiilu Nyasha, becuz freedom *is* a constant struggle, N'Gugi wa Thiongo, Dr. Chinosole, Dr. Hussein Abdilahi Bulhan, Dr. Ernest P. Keen, Dr. Frances Cress Welsing, Dr. Frantz Fanon; to one who escaped the slave coffle and became two—Dhoruba and Tanaquil; to men and women who are no longer Panthers but are still rumbling—Safiya Bukhari-Alston, the late Nat Shanks, Capt. Reggie Schell, Emory Douglas, Harold Jamison, Rosemari Mealy, Linda Richardson, and those who never apologized for wearing the black beret. To Frances Goldin, who reached into the storm and pulled out this tome; to Noelle Hanrahan who brought in the deadliest of weapons behind the walls—a tape recorder! To Jane and Alexander; to my bros. across this country; to the many good folks who remained unnamed but not unknown. To the vast extended family that is the brood of Edith—Keith, Lydia, Basil Ali, Wayne, William, and their/her growing progeny; Flutenjuice, Jaleel, Jamal, Tifa, Nyabinta, Jabari, Wayne and Mazimu; to Marilyn and Habibah who fed that brood with their love.

And lastly, but not leastly, to my wife Mydiya Wadiya Jamal, and the entire Jamal clan, to all my Ibns and Bintas, gifts from the divine Source who revealed the face of love in human form.

Preface

Don't tell me about the valley of the shadow of death. I live there. In south-central Pennsylvania's Huntingdon County a one-hundred-year-old prison stands, its Gothic towers projecting an air of foreboding, evoking a gloomy mood of the Dark Ages. I and some seventy-eight other men spend about twenty-two hours a day in six- by ten-foot cells.* The additional two hours may be spent outdoors, in a chain-link-fenced box, ringed by concertina razor wire, under the gaze of gun turrets.

Welcome to Pennsylvania's death row.

---

* Pennsylvania Department of Corrections Persons in the State Correctional System Sentenced to Execution as of December 20, 1994.

Note: In December 1994 the Pennsylvania Department of Corrections began transferring death row inmates to SCI Greene County, a new supermaximum (or control unit) prison which is expected to house the vast majority of Pennsylvania death row inmates. Mumia was transferred there on January 13, 1995.

I'm a bit stunned. Several years ago the Pennsylvania Supreme Court affirmed my conviction and sentence of death, by a vote of four justices (three did not participate). As a black journalist who was a Black Panther way back in my yon teens, I've often studied America's long history of legal lynchings of Africans. I remember a front page of the *Black Panther* newspaper, bearing the quote "A black man has no rights that a white man is bound to respect," attributed to U.S. Supreme Court chief justice Roger Taney, of the infamous *Dred Scott* case,* where America's highest court held that neither Africans nor their "free" descendants are entitled to the rights of the Constitution. Deep, huh? It's true.

Perhaps I'm naive, maybe I'm just stupid— but I thought the law would be followed in my case, and the conviction reversed. Really.

Even in the face of the brutal Philadelphia MOVE† massacre of May 13, 1985, that led to Ramona Africa's frame-up, Eleanor Bumpurs, Mi-

---

* *Dred Scott v. Sanford* 19 U.S. (How.) 393, 407, 15 L.Ed. 691 (1857).
† "The MOVE organization surfaced in Philadelphia during the early 70's. Characterized by dreadlock hair, the adopted surname 'Africa,' a principled unity, and an uncompromising commitment to their belief. Members practice the teachings of MOVE founder *John Africa.*" From *Twenty Years on a Move.*

chael Stewart, Clement Lloyd, Allan Blanchard, and countless other police slaughters of blacks from New York to Miami, with impunity, my faith remained. Even in the face of this relentless wave of antiblack state terror, *I thought my appeals would be successful.* I still harbored a belief in U.S. law, and the realization that my appeal had been denied was a shocker. I could understand intellectually that American courts are reservoirs of racist sentiment and have historically been hostile to black defendants, but a lifetime of propaganda about American "justice" is hard to shrug off.

I need but look across the nation, where, as of December 1994, blacks constituted some 40 percent of men on death row,* or across Pennsylvania, where, as of December 1994, 111 of 184 men on death row—over 60%—are black, to see the truth, a truth hidden under black robes† and promises of equal rights. Blacks constitute just over 9 percent of Pennsylvania's population and just under 11 percent of America's.‡

---

* *Death Row USA*, NAACP Legal Defense and Education Fund, Fall 1994.

† Pennsylvania Department of Corrections Persons in the State Correctional System Sentenced to Execution as of December 20, 1994.

‡ Census Profile Race and Hispanic Origin. Profile No. 2, June 1991. Bureau of Census, U.S. Department.

As I said, it's hard to shrug off, but maybe we can do it together. How? Try out this quote I saw in a 1982 law book, by a prominent Philadelphia lawyer named David Kairys: "Law is simply politics by other means."* Such a line goes far to explain how courts really function, whether today, or 138 years ago in the *Scott* case. It ain't about "law," it's about "politics" by "other means." Now, ain't that the truth?

I continue to fight against this unjust sentence and conviction. Perhaps we can shrug off and shred some of the dangerous myths laid on our minds like a second skin—such as the "right" to a fair and impartial jury of our peers; the "right" to represent oneself; the "right" to a fair trial, even. They're *not* rights—they're privileges of the powerful and rich. For the powerless and the poor, they are chimera that vanish once one reaches out to claim them as something real or substantial. Don't expect the media networks to tell you, for they can't, because of the incestuousness between the media and the

---

* D. Kairys, *Legal Reasoning in Politics of Law*, D. Kairys, ed. 1982 24 16–17. From Foley, M.A., *Critical Legal Studies* 91 *Dickinson Law Review* 467, at 473 (Winter 1986).

government, and big business, which they both serve.

I can.

Even if I must do so from the valley of the shadow of death, I will.

From death row, this is Mumia Abu-Jamal.

December 1994

Introduction

John Edgar Wideman

Recalling the horrors of African-American history, accepting the challenges our history presently places on us, is like acknowledging a difficult, unpleasant duty or debt that's been hanging over our heads a very long time, an obligation that we know in our hearts we must deal with but that we keep putting off and evading, as if one day procrastination will make the burden, the obligation we must undertake, disappear.

Mumia Abu-Jamal forces us to confront the burden of our history. In one of his columns from death row he quotes at length an 1857 ruling of the U.S. Supreme Court. The issue being determined by the Court is whether the descendants of slaves, when they shall be emancipated, are full citizens of the United States. Chief Justice Roger Taney states:

> We think they are not, and that they were not included, and were not intended to be included, under the word "citizens" in the Constitution, and can therefore claim none of the rights and privileges of the United States. . . .
>
> [A] perpetual and impossible barrier was intended to be erected between the white race and the one which they had reduced to slavery, and governed as subjects with absolute and despotic power, and which they then looked upon as so far below them in the scale of created beings, that intermarriages between white persons and negroes or mulattoes were regarded as unnatural and immoral, and punished as crimes.*

Justice Taney, speaking for the Court, confirms the judgment of his ancestors and articulates an attitude prevailing to this very day.

Mumia points out that Thurgood Marshall, the first person of African descent appointed to the U.S. Supreme Court, admitted, just hours

---

* *Dred Scott v. Sanford* 19 U.S. (19 How.) 393, 15 L. Ed. 691 (1856).

after his resignation from the Court, that "I'm still not free."*

In another essay, Mumia calls our attention to Nelson Mandela. Released after twenty-seven years in South Africa's jails as a political prisoner, Mandela—honored, celebrated as a hero, leader, and liberator of his people, universally acknowledged to be the most powerful man in his country, its best hope for peace, possibly its next president—still didn't possess the right to vote.

Mumia Abu-Jamal's writing insists on these kinds of gut checks, reality checks. He reminds us that to move clearly in the present, we must understand the burden of our past.

Situated as he is in prison, a prison inside a prison actually, since he's confined on death row, Mumia Abu-Jamal's day-to-day life would seem to share little with ours, out here in the so-called free world. Then again, if we think a little deeper, we might ask ourselves—who isn't on death row? Perhaps one measure of humanity is

---

* Justice Marshall's June 28, 1991, press conference on his retirement from the U.S. Supreme Court, Federal News Service transcript.

our persistence in the business of attempting to construct a meaningful life in spite of the sentence of death hanging over our heads every instant of our time on earth.

Although we can't avoid our inevitable mortality, we don't need to cower in a corner, waiting for annihilation. Neither should we allow the seemingly overwhelming evil news of the day to freeze us in our tracks, nor let it become an excuse for doing nothing, for denial and avoidance, for hiding behind imaginary walls and pretending nothing can harm us.

Alternatives exist. Struggle exists. Struggle to connect, to imagine ourselves better. To imagine a better world. To take responsibility step by step, day by day, for changing the little things we can control, refusing to accept the large things that appear out of control. The life and the essays of Mumia Abu-Jamal provide us with models for struggle.

In 1981, to connect with my younger brother who was serving a life term without parole in a Pennsylvania prison, I wrote a book with him called *Brothers and Keepers*. In my research for the book I discovered a chilling fact. My country, the

United States of America, ranked third among the nations of the world in the percentage of its citizens it imprisoned. Only Russia and South Africa surpassed us.

Who would have guessed that, thirteen years later, the powerful governments of two of the top three incarcerating nations would have been overturned by internal revolutions. We're number one now. And in spite of the warning implicit in the fate of governments that choose repression over reform, we're building more prisons as fast as we can.

The facile notion of incarceration as a cure for social, economic, and political problems has usurped the current national discussion of these issues. As I traveled from city to city on a book tour last fall, the dominant issue dramatized in TV campaign ads coast to coast was: Which candidate is tougher on crime.

During the same tour, a hot story in national and local newspapers, on TV news, talk shows, and radio call-ins was the IQ controversy occasioned by the publication of several books claiming that the innate intelligence of blacks was lower than that of whites. Why such widespread, excited coverage of this hoary topic?

That some people believe black folk are born inferior to whites, and thus genetically determined to occupy the lowest rung of society certainly isn't news. Neither is blaming the victim of oppression, a strategy with a history at least as ancient as Europe's slave trading in Africa. I recall sitting on college admissions committees thirty years ago and hearing many of those who are voicing the idea of black mental inferiority today singing the same song then to rationalize underrepresentation of African-Americans in higher education.

So the fact that some *experts* continue to believe in innate black inferiority (or proclaim it without truly believing, since they must know that the basic terms in the debate—race and intelligence—are problematic at best, malicious fictions at worst, and know a mountain of tables, graphs, statistics, and experiments can neither affirm nor deny premises and assumptions themselves imprecise and untestable, *how many angels can fit on the head of a pin*) is not news. Rather, the IQ controversy is an ominous sign of misinformation and repression going hand in hand. Exterminating Jews becomes easier if you're able to provide sound "scientific" reasons for pogroms.

Postulating a biologically determined IQ deficit in blacks is more than malicious mischief. It is a transparent ploy to justify (and erase from the national consciousness) thirty years of backsliding from the promise of equality exacted by the civil rights movement of the 1960s.

For African-Americans the backsliding has created a slightly larger black middle class on one hand, and on the other a growing underclass of people of color trapped on the bottom rung of an economic ladder without any more rungs. For white Americans, reneging on the promise of equality has engendered class stratification and polarization just as severe as among blacks. On the bottom, the stagnant poverty of unemployment, welfare, poor education, and transience infect more and more of those who once considered themselves working people with dignity and aspirations. In the middle a rapidly shrinking majority beset by fear, trembling, and anger. They know they are walking a tightrope—away from unforgiving poverty, toward a mirage of boundless wealth that confers immunity from hard times. A tightrope, they also know in their hearts, leads nowhere—unless they hit the lottery—except to more stressful, precarious steps along the razor's edge or a sudden, precipitous fall. Finally, at the top stands a tiny minority whose wealth is a wall protecting them from the chaos of social instability, a wall that is both a reaction to the moral chaos of inequality and dependent on it.

We face a social landscape with more (or at least as much) need for radical change than we faced in the 1960s, an era that produced, flawed though it was by lack of follow-through, a mighty impulse toward change. Yet today the opposite impulse drives us. Walls separating Americans by race, gender, class, and region are being justified and celebrated, but not in a spirit that welcomes diversity or seeks ultimate unity through mutual respect and reconciliation. Prison walls are being proposed as a final solution. They symbolize our shortsightedness, our fear of the real problems caging us all. The pity is how blindly, enthusiastically, we applaud those who are constructing the walls dooming us.

Mumia Abu-Jamal's voice is considered dangerous and subversive and thus is censored from National Public Radio, to name just one influential medium. Many books about black people, including a slew of briskly selling biographies and autobiographies—from Oprah to O.J. to Maya Angelou—are on the stands. What sets Mumia's story apart as so threatening?

It is useful to remember that the slave narrative and its progeny, the countless up-from-the-depths biographies and autobiographies of black people that repeat the form and assumptions of the slave narrative, have always been best-sellers. They encapsulate one of the master plots Americans have found acceptable for black lives. These neoslave narratives carry a message the majority of people wealthy enough to purchase books wish to hear.

The message consists of a basic *deep structure* repeated in a seemingly endless variety of packages and voices. The slave narratives of the 1800s posited and then worked themselves out in a bifurcated, either/or world. The action of the story concerns moving from one world to another. The actor is a single individual, a featured star, and we watch and listen as this protagonist undergoes his or her rite of passage. South to north, rural to urban, black environment (plantation) to white environment (everywhere, including the language in which the narrator converses with the reader), silence to literacy, are some of the classic crossovers accomplished by the protagonists of such fables. If you punch in modern variants of these dichotomies—ghetto to middle class, ignorance to education, unskilled to professional, despised gangster to enlightened spokesperson, you can see how persistent and malleable the formula is.

The formula for the neoslave narrative sells because it is simple; because it accepts and maintains the categories (black/white, for instance) of the status quo; because it is about individuals, not groups, crossing boundaries; because it comforts and consoles those in power and offers a ray of hope to the powerless. Although the existing social arrangements may allow the horrors of plantations, ghettos, and prisons to exist, the narratives tell us, these arrangements also allow room for some to escape. Thus the arrangements are not absolutely evil. No one is absolutely guilty, nor are the oppressed (slave, prisoner, ghetto inhabitant) absolutely guiltless. If some overcome, why don't the others?

Vicarious identification with the narrator's harrowing adventures, particularly if the tale is told in first person "I," permits readers to have their cake and eat it too. They experience the chill and thrill of being an outsider. In the safety of an armchair, readers can root for the crafty slave as the slave pits himself against an outrageously evil system that legitimizes human bondage. Readers can ignore for a charmed moment their reliance on the same system to pay for the book, the armchair.

The neoslave narratives thus serve the ambivalent function of their ancestors. The fate of one black individual is foregrounded, removed from the network of systemic relationships connecting, defining, determining, undermining all American lives. This manner of viewing black lives at best ignores, at worst reinforces, an apartheid status quo. Divisive categories that structure the world of the narratives—slave/free, black/white, underclass/middle class, female/male—are not interrogated. The idea of a collective, intertwined fate recedes. The mechanisms of class, race, and gender we have inherited are perpetuated ironically by a genre purporting to illustrate the possibility of breaking barriers and transcending the conditions into which one is born.

Mumia Abu-Jamal's essays question matters left untouched by most of the popular stories of black lives decorating bookstores today. And therein lies much of the power, the urgency, of his writing.

His essays are important as departure and corrective. He examines the place where he is—*prison*, his status—*prisoner, black man*, but refuses to accept the notion of difference and separation these labels project. Although he yearns for freedom, demands freedom, he does not identify freedom with release from prison, does not confuse freedom with what his jailers can give or take away, does not restrict the concept of freedom to the world beyond the bars his jailers enter from each day. Although dedicated to personal liberation, he envisions that liberation as partially dependent on the collective fate of black people. He doesn't split his world down the middle to conform to the divided world prison enforces. He expresses the necessity of connection, relinquishing to no person or group the power to define him. His destiny, his manhood, is not attached to some desperate, one-way urge to cross over to a region controlled or possessed by others. What he is, who he can become, results from his daily struggle to construct an identity wherever his circumstances place him.

Isn't one of the lessons of African-American culture the reality of an unseen world, below, above, around, what is visible? Our history offers witness to the fact that our living, our art, and our spirits can prosper in the face of the most extreme physical deprivation. Aren't Mumia Abu-Jamal's words reaching us now, in spite of steel bars and a death sentence, another instance of our capacity to keep on keeping on?

The first truth Mumia tells us is that he ain't dead yet. And although his voice is vital and strong, he assures us it ain't because nobody ain't trying to kill him and shut him up. In fact, just the opposite is true. The power of his voice is rooted in his defiance of those determined to silence him. Magically, Mumia's words are clarified and purified by the toxic strata of resistance through which they must penetrate to reach us. Like the blues. Like jazz.

Remember the fairy tale about the emperor's new clothes, how a kid blurts out "He's naked" as the emperor struts past, decked out in his illusory splendor? What ever happened to the kid who spoiled the emperor's show? Consider what has happened to black men—Martin, Malcolm, Mandela—who have shouted out "He's naked." If the fairy tale were set in an American city today and the child cast as a black boy, we know he'd be shot or locked up or both. Nobody wants to hear the bad news, the truth exposing the empire's self-delusions, especially those who profit most from the delusions.

Chinua Achebe, the great Nigerian novelist, teaches us that the poet and the king must never become too friendly because the poet's job is to bear to the people unglad tidings the king would just as soon nobody hears.

The best slave narratives and prison narratives have always asked profound questions, implicitly and explicitly, about the meaning of a life. Part of the work of blues, jazz, our best artistic endeavors, is (thank you, Mr. Ellison) *to reveal the chaos which lives within the pattern of our certainties*. In a new world where African people were transported to labor, die, and disappear, we've needed unbound voices to reformulate our destiny— voices refusing to be ensnared by somebody else's terms. We've developed the knack of finding such voices in the oddest, darkest, most unforeseen places. A chorus of them exists in Great Time, the seamless medium uniting past, present, and future. The voices are always there, if we discipline ourselves to pick them out. Listen to them, to ourselves, to the best we've managed to write and say and dance and paint and sing. African-American culture, in spite of the weight, the assaults it has endured, may contain a key to our nation's survival, a key not found simply in the goal of material prosperity, but in the force of spirit, will, communal interdependence.

Because he tells the truth, Mumia Abu-Jamal's voice can help us tear down walls—prison walls, the walls we hide behind to deny and refuse the burden of our history.

part one

Life on death row

Teetering on the brink between life and death

> For there to be equivalence, the death penalty would have to punish a criminal who had warned his victim of the date at which he would inflict a horrible death on him and who, from that moment onward, had confined him at his mercy for months. Such a monster is not encountered in private life.
>
> —*Albert Camus**

"Yard in!"

The last yard of the day is finally called. "Capitals! Fourth, fifth, and sixth tier—YARD UP!" the corpulent correctional officer bellows, his rural accent alien to the urban ear.

One by one, cells are unlocked for the daily

---

* From *Reflections on the Guillotine*, in *Resistance, Rebellion, and Death*, 199, O'Brien translation 1961, posthumous collection of essays.

3

trek from cell to cage. Each man is pat-searched by guards armed with batons and then scanned by a metal detector.

Once the inmates are encaged, the midsummer sky rumbles, its dark clouds swell, pregnant with power and water. A bespectacled white-shirt turns his pale face skyward, examining nature's quickening portent. The rumbles grow louder as drops of rain sail earthward, splattering steel, brick, and human.

"Yard in!" the white-shirt yells, sparking murmurs of resentment among the men.

"Yard in?! Shit, man, we just got out here!"

The guards adopt a cajoling, rather than threatening, attitude. "C'mon, fellas—yard in, yard in. Ya know we can't leave y'uns out here when it gits ta thunderin' an' lightnin'."

"Oh, why not? Y'all 'fraid we gonna get ourself electrocuted?" a prisoner asks.

"Ain't that a bitch?" another adds. "They must be afraid that if we do get electrocuted by lightnin', they won't have no jobs and won't get paid!"

A few guffaws, and the trail from cage to cell thickens.

Although usually two hours long, today's yard barely lasts ten minutes, for fear that those con-

4

demned to death by the state may perish, instead, by fate.

For approximately twenty-four hundred people locked in state and federal prisons, life is unlike that in any other institution. These are America's condemned, who bear a stigma far worse than "prisoner." These are America's death row residents: men and women who walk the razor's edge between half-life and certain death in thirty-four states or under the jurisdiction of the United States. The largest death row stands in Texas (324 people: 120 African-Americans, 144 whites, 52 Hispanics, 4 Native Americans, and 4 Asian-Americans); the smallest are in Connecticut (2 whites), New Mexico (1 Native American, 1 white), and Wyoming (2 whites).*

You will find a blacker world on death row than anywhere else. African-Americans, a mere 11 percent of the national population, compose about 40 percent of the death row population. There, too, you will find this writer.

---

* Statistics are as of January 1991. As of October 1994, the United States has 2948 people on death row. The largest death row is in California (396), followed by Texas (390), and Florida (349), and Pennsylvania (168). This information is from *Death Row USA*, NAACP/Legal Defense and Education Fund, Fall 1994.

Control

It is from Pennsylvania's largest death row at the State Correctional Institute at Huntingdon, in rural south-central Pennsylvania, that I write. In the Commonwealth I am but one of 123 persons who await death. I have lived in this barren domain of death since the summer of 1983. For several years now I have been assigned DC (disciplinary custody) status for daring to abide by my faith, the teachings of *John Africa*, and, in particular, for refusing to cut my hair.* For this I have been denied family phone calls, and on occasion I have been shackled for refusing to violate my beliefs.

Life here oscillates between the banal and the bizarre.

Unlike other prisoners, death row inmates are not "doing time." Freedom does not shine at the end of the tunnel. Rather, the end of the tunnel brings extinction. Thus, for many here, there is no hope.

---

* Mumia Abu-Jamal is off "DC" (disciplinary custody) status, but he remains on "AC" (administrative custody) status, as are all Pennsylvania death row inmates, and hence restricted.

6

As in any massive, quasi-military organization, reality on the row is regimented by rule and regulation. As against any regime imposed on human personality, there is resistance, but far less than one might expect. For the most part, death row prisoners are the best behaved and least disruptive of all inmates. It also is true, however, that we have little opportunity to be otherwise, given that many death units operate on the "22 + 2" system: 22 hours locked in cell, followed by 2 hours of recreation out of cell. Outdoor recreation takes place in a cage, ringed with double-edged razor wire—the "dog pen."

All death rows share a central goal: "human storage" in an "austere world in which condemned prisoners are treated as bodies kept alive to be killed."* Pennsylvania's death row regime is among America's most restrictive, rivaling the

---

* Johnson and Carroll, "Litigating Death Row Conditions: The Case for Reform," in *Prisoners and the Law*, 8-3, 8-5; I. Robbins ed. 1988; quoting R. Johnson, "Death Row Confinement: The Psychological and Moral Issues" 5 (unpublished paper presented in colloquium on the death penalty at Towson State University, March 10, 1983).

Note: SCI Greene, Pennsylvania's new death row, confines prisoners to solitary confinement twenty-four hours a day, two days per week, and twenty-three hours per day the other five days: A mere five hours of recreation per week.

7

infamous San Quentin death unit for the intensity and duration of restriction. A few states allow four, six, or even eight hours out of cell, prison employment, or even access to educational programs. Not so in the Keystone State.

Here one has little or no psychological life. Here many escape death's omnipresent specter only by way of common diversions—television, radio, or sports. TVs are allowed, but not typewriters: one's energies may be expended freely on entertainment, but a tool essential for one's liberation through judicial process is deemed a security risk.

One inmate, more interested in his life than his entertainment, argued forcefully with prison administrators for permission to buy a nonimpact, nonmetallic, battery-operated typewriter. Predictably, permission was denied for security reasons. "Well, what do y'all consider a thirteen-inch piece of glass?" the prisoner asked. "Ain't that a security risk?"

"Where do you think you'll get that from?" the prison official demanded.

"From my TV!"

Request for typewriter denied.

*   *   *

TV is more than a powerful diversion from a terrible fate. It is a psychic club used to threaten those who dare resist the dehumanizing isolation of life on the row. To be found guilty of an institutional infraction means that one must relinquish TV.

After months or years of noncontact visits, few phone calls, and ever decreasing communication with one's family and others, many inmates use TV as an umbilical cord, a psychological connection to the world they have lost. They depend on it, in the way that lonely people turn to TV for the illusion of companionship, and they dread separation from it. For many, loss of TV is too high a price to pay for any show of resistance.

Humiliation

Visits are an exercise in humiliation.

In Pennsylvania, as in many other death states, noncontact visits are the rule. It is not just a security rule; it is a policy and structure that attempts to sever emotional connection by denying physical connection between the visitor and the inmate. Visits are conducted in a closed room, roughly eighty square feet in size. The prisoner is handcuffed and separated by a partition of shatterproof glass, steel trim, and wire mesh.

What visitors do not see, prior to the visit, is a horrifying spectacle—the body-cavity strip search. Once the prisoner is naked, the visiting-room guard spits out a familiar cadence:

"Open yer mouth.

Stick out your tongue.

You wear any dentures?

Lemme see both sides of your hands.

Pull your foreskin back.

Lift your sac.

Turn around.

Bend over.

Spread your cheeks.

Bottom of yer feet.

Get dressed."

Several prisoners have protested to the administration that such searches are unreasonable, arguing that body-cavity strip searches before and after noncontact visits cannot be justified. Either allow contact visits, they argue, or halt the body-cavity strip searches. But prison officials have responded to this proposal as they have to repeated calls by the condemned for allowance of typewriters: refusal, due to security risk.

For the visitor, too, such visits are deeply disturbing.

In *Rhem v. Malcolm*, the often-cited case on prison conditions in New York, Judge Lasker quoted expert testimony from Karl Menninger, the late psychiatrist, who described noncontact visiting as "the most unpleasant and most disturbing detail in the whole prison," and a practice that constitutes "a violation of ordinary principles of humanity." Dr. Menninger stated: "[I]t's such a painful sight that I don't stay but a minute or two as a rule. It's a painful thing. . . . I feel so sorry for them, so ashamed of myself that I get out of the room."*

The ultimate effect of noncontact visits is to weaken, and finally to sever, family ties. Through this policy and practice the state skillfully and intentionally denies those it condemns a fundamental element and expression of humanity—that of touch and physical contact— and thereby slowly erodes family ties already

---

* *Rhem v. Malcolm* 371 F. supp. 594 (1974); 527 F.2d 1041 (1975).

11

made tenuous by the distance between home and prison. Thus prisoners are as isolated psychologically as they are temporally and spatially. By state action, they become "dead" to those who know and love them, and therefore dead to themselves. For who are people, but for their relations and relationships?

Hurled by judicial decree into this netherworld of despair, forcefully separated from relationships, overcome by the dual shame of their station and the circumstances of the crime that led them to death's door, a few succumb to the shady release of suicide. Some fight Sisyphian battles, struggling to prove their innocence and reverse unjust convictions. Others live as they are treated—as "shadows of [their] former selves, in a pantomime of life, human husks."*

To such men and women, the actual execution is a fait accompli, a formality already accomplished in spirit, where the state concludes its premeditated drama by putting the "dead" to death a second time.

---

* Johnson and Carroll, op. cit.

Politics and "justice" of death

Although it might be said fairly that many people, both in and outside of prison, are utterly uninformed as to the workings of the U.S. Supreme Court, some among those on death row watch the Court with acute attention. For them, the sudden resignation of Justice William J. Brennan, Jr., comes as crushing news after a season of sorrow. The recent spate of losses suffered by capital litigators spells all but certain doom for those who continue to petition the present Court for legal relief.

Where the issue of the death penalty is concerned, law follows politics, and conservatives won the sociopolitical battles of the 1980s on the basis of an agenda that included a ringing endorsement of capital punishment. The venerated principle of *stare decisis*—following rulings of previous judicial decisions—meant little in the politically charged judicial arena. Statistical methodology and scientific and sociological studies, once valued tools for challenging state practice, now serve as meaningless academic exercises.

McCleskey v. Kemp (1987)* was the clincher. The Supreme Court majority, Justice Powell writing, assumed the validity of the so-called Baldus study,† which presented mounds of powerful statistical data demonstrating gross racial disparity in Georgia's death penalty tallies, but rejected the study's clear implications.

Justice Brennan's dissent telescoped the Baldus study's meaning: defendants charged with killing whites are 4.3 times more likely to be sentenced to die than defendants charged with killing blacks; six of every eleven defendants convicted of killing a white would not have received a death sentence had their victim been black. Thus the study showed that "there was a significant chance that race would play a prominent role in determining if [a defendant] lived or died."

The majority's perambulations to its eventual rejection of that which it could hardly deny—that the race of the victim is a primary factor in determining whether a defendant lives or dies—

---

* *McCleskey v. Kemp* 481 U.S. 279 (1987).
† *The Baldus Study*, Baldus, Pulaski, and Woodworth, "Comparative Review of Death Sentences: An Empirical Study of Georgia Experience," 74 J. Crim. L. and C. (1983)

proved the potency of the old adage offered by the satirical character Mr. Dooley,* who shrewdly observed: "No matter whether th' constitution follows th' flag or not, th' supreme coort follows th' iliction returns."

McCleskey's claim, based on sophisticated statistical and multiple regression analyses, buttressed by "our understanding of history and human experience,"† was not disproved by the *McCleskey* Court; rather, it was rejected out of fear. In rejecting the conclusion that the facts established an unconstitutional infirmity, Justice Powell noted with alarm that "McCleskey's claim, taken to its logical conclusion, throws into serious question the principles that underlie our entire criminal justice system."‡

Precisely.

Because McCleskey dared question the fundamental fairness of the entire system, his claims were answered with rejection.

---

* F. Dunne, *The Supreme Court's Decisions* in Mr. Dooley on the Choice of Law 47, 52 (E. Bander ed. 1963); collection of newspaper essays from the turn of the century.

† From Justice William Brennan's dissent in the case *McCleskey v. Kemp* 481 U.S. 279 (1987); quote verbatim from dissent.

‡ From Justice Powell in *McCleskey v. Kemp*; quote verbatim.

Delbert Tibbs, an African-American divinity student, once found himself tossed in with death row prisoners in Florida. Convicted by an all-white jury in 1974 for a rape and related murder, he spent three harrowing years in death's shadow before appellate reversal.

In speaking about his jury, he observed:

PEER: one of equal rank; one among equals. I knew the definition of that word, and there was nothing remotely akin to this meaning existing between me and these seven hard-eyed White Men and five cold-eyed White Women who made up this jury of my "peers."

I knew that any peerage that they comprised, as indeed they did comprise such a thing, totally excluded me, at least, in *their* eyes. . . .

Peers, indeed.

I'm sure that in the eyes of that jury I was not *just another* human being. Oh, no. I was dangerous, because, darker. I didn't belong. . . .

On the McCleskey decision, Tibbs noted:

Apparently, that Justice of the United States, writing for the majority, thinks that the United States is

not two separate societies, one black and one white, and quite unequal. . . .

Justice is not meted out without regard to race, sex, economics, or previous condition of servitude. . . .

That Justice was speaking as if there were no Civil War and no chattel slavery. He spoke as if there were no history of lynchings, as if there were no Dred Scott decision, no Medgar Evers, Little Rock, nor "Bombingham." Memphis didn't happen in that America.*

What does happen, in this America, is the cheapening of black life and the placing of a premium on white life. As Justice Brennan's eloquent dissent in *McCleskey* argues, the fact that this practice may be customary does not make it constitutional.

To do justice, one must consistently battle, in Brennan's words, "a fear of too much justice." Finding that fear firmly entrenched, he framed his arguments not merely as counters to positions with which he passionately disagreed, but also as warnings for the future, a day not yet dawned:

* Delbert Tibbs, "From Seminary to Cell Block," in *A Saga of Shame: Racial Discrimination and the Death Penalty*, 16, 17; publication of Quixote Center, 1989.

It is tempting to pretend that minorities on death row share a fate in no way connected to our own, that our treatment of them sounds no echoes beyond the chambers in which they die. Such an illusion is ultimately corrosive, for the reverberations of injustice are not so easily confined. . . .

The Court's decision today will not change what attorneys in Georgia tell other Warren McCleskeys about their chances of execution. Nothing will soften the harsh message they must convey, nor alter the prospect that race undoubtedly will continue to be a topic of discussion. McCleskey's evidence will not have obtained judicial acceptance, but that will not affect what is said on death row. However many criticisms of today's decision may be rendered, these painful conversations will serve as the most eloquent dissents of all.*

Ironically, perhaps, the "eloquent dissents" of *pro se*† Court-watchers are commonly delivered in the winning or losing of a bet: inmates on the row often wager with one another on the outcome of judicial decisions. But as the real stakes

---

* Justice William Brennan's dissent in the case *McCleskey v. Kemp*, 481 U.S. 279 (1987).

† Definition of *pro se*: to act as his or her own attorney.

riding on any given outcome are high, objective predictions are rarely possible.

By viewing every decision through the prism of politics, I never lost a bet—even in cases where jailhouse lawyers claimed to have the law on their side. There is, of course, no satisfaction in such victories: every bet won has been a case lost; every case lost, a step closer to death. My predictions, based on political winds rather than law, have earned me the enmity of those jailhouse lawyers who continue to place faith in legal precedents and principles despite their growing pile of lost wagers.

Death march and lessons unlearned

There is a quickening on the nation's death rows of late—a picking up of the pace of the march toward death. The political prod is sparking movement, and judges in death cases are beginning to find themselves under increasing pressure to make the final judgment.

As murder rates rise in American cities, so too does the tide of fear. Both politicians and judges continue to ride that tide that washes toward the execution chamber's door. No matter that of the ten states with the highest murder rate, eight lead the country in executions that supposedly deter; no matter that of the ten states with the lowest murder rate, only one (Utah) has executed anyone since 1976. No matter that the effectiveness of the death penalty is not really debated; no matter that the contention that the death penalty makes citizens safer is no longer seriously argued.

Habeas corpus,* fundamental to English law since the reign of King Charles and to the U.S. Constitution since its inception, now faces evisceration under the hand of the chief justice of the Supreme Court, a possibility unthinkable just a few years ago. Many of the condemned, with constitutional error rife throughout their records, will soon be executed without meaningful review.

States that have not slain in a generation now ready their machinery: generators whine, poison liquids are mixed, gases are measured and read-

---

* Definition of *habeas corpus*: a broad writ where anyone who is unlawfully incarcerated can petition any state or federal court in an attempt to obtain their freedom. A means by which state prisoners can bring constitutionally based challenges of their convictions before the federal courts.

ied, silent chambers await the order to smother life. Increasingly, America's northern states now join the rushing pack, anxious to relink themselves with their pre-*Furman** heritage.

Deterrence? The March 1988 execution of Willie Darden in Florida, exceedingly well publicized here and abroad, should have had enormous deterrent effect, according to capital theories. But less than eleven hours after two thousand volts coursed through Darden's manacled flesh, a Florida corrections officer, well positioned to absorb and understand the lessons of the state ritual, erupted in a jealous rage and murdered a man in the maternity wing of a hospital.[†]

Seems like a lesson well learned to me.

Yale Law Journal *January 1991*

---

* *Furman v. Georgia*, 408 U.S. 238 (1972); imposition and carrying out of death penalty in cases before the Court would constitute cruel and unusual punishment in violation of Eighth and Fourteenth Amendments.

[†] Breslin, "State Shouldn't Be in the Killing Business," *The Sunday News* (Lancaster, PA), March 20, 1988, A15.

Descent into hell

The man sat with arm shackled to the steel grille.

A passing glance told much of the tale, a story of utter, total alienation, written in every line wrinkled in his pale face. His white, unstriped jumpsuit revealed the prison's assignment of the man to the so-called psychiatric observation unit. His inability, or unwillingness, to have eye contact with the men around him suggested avoidance. His tremors and his repetitive, rapid hand and leg clinches and other movements told a darker story: that of heavy or long-term use of powerful psychotropic drugs, such as Thorazine, Stelazine, or Haldol, a side effect of which is tardive dyskinesia—a condition that renders its sufferers prey to a wild variety of inappropriate body tics and shakings. The spark? Powerful, mind-bending drugs, prescribed to prisoners liberally, especially in light of a recent U.S.

Supreme Court ruling that allows prison officials free rein to drug prisoners insensate.

The older prisoner with whom I was walking nodded in the man's direction.

"Check that guy out!"

"I saw him, man."

"He plenty messed up!"

"You're right—but he ain't gonna get no help here."

The brief exchange was shelved, with no apparent reason for recall later.

A day later, during the midday meal, the unmistakable odor of burnt hair drifted sharply around the block.

"Somebody burnin' they hair, man! You smell that?"

"I smell it, but that ain't hair—that's a blanket."

"Blanket, hell. That's hair, man—human hair! Fire up!" Big Boy bellowed until others took up the call: "Fire up! Fire up!"

For five frantic minutes the call resounded, and guards, the ever-present keys ajangle, ran from cell to cell, from tier to tier, until the burning, smoking cell was located and the white frothy liquid quenched the flames.

Moments later, a naked man walked down the

tier, his front darkened like wheat toast, an acrid stench rising like an infernal sacrifice. He walked slowly, deliberately, as if lost in thought, as if involved in a languid, aimless stroll on the beach.

Twelve hours later he was pronounced dead, with over 70 percent of his body burned.

He was identified as Robert Barnes, fifty-seven years old, of Delaware County, Pennsylvania. A recent transfer from Graterford prison to Huntingdon prison, the man had reportedly warned officials that if he were placed in the "hole" (disciplinary custody status) and locked down, he would kill himself.

He was placed in the "hole."

He killed himself.

Although he had an extensive psychiatric history, and had made a recent suicide threat, he was placed in a strip cell for twenty-four hours a day. When he was found, his burned jumpsuit had been totally consumed.

Like many long-term prisoners in Pennsylvania with serious psychiatric and mental problems, Huntingdon's "hole" became a way station for a descent into hell.

December 1990

The visit

In the midst of darkness, this little one was a light ray. Tiny, with a Minnie Mouse voice, this daughter of my spirit had finally made the long trek westward, into the bowels of this man-made hell, situated in the south-central Pennsylvania boondocks. She, like my other children, was just a baby when I was cast into hell, and because of her youth and sensitivity, she hadn't been brought along on family visits until now.

She burst into the tiny visiting room, her brown eyes aglitter with happiness; stopped, stunned, staring at the glassy barrier between us; and burst into tears at this arrogant attempt at state separation. In milliseconds, sadness and shock shifted into fury as her petite fingers curled into tight fists, which banged and pummeled the Plexiglas barrier, which shuddered and shimmied but didn't shatter.

"Break it! Break it!" she screamed. Her mother, recovering from her shock, bundled up Hamida in her arms, as sobs rocked them both. My eyes filled to the brim. My nose clogged.

Her unspoken words echoed in my consciousness: "Why *can't* I hug him? Why *can't* we kiss? Why *can't* I sit in his lap? *Why can't we touch?* Why not?" I turned away to recover.

I put on a silly face, turned back, called her to me, and talked silly to her. "Girl, how can you breathe with all them boogies in your nose?" Amid the rolling trail of tears, a twinkle started like dawn, and before long the shy beginnings of a smile meandered across her face as we talked silly talk.

I reminded her of how she used to hug our cat until she almost strangled the poor animal, and Hamida's denials were developing into laughter. The three of us talked silly talk, liberally mixed with serious talk, and before long our visit came to an end. Her smile restored, she uttered a parting poem that we used to say over the phone: "I love you, I miss you, and when I see you, I'm gonna kiss you!" The three of us laughed and they left.

Over five years have passed since that visit, but

I remember it like it was an hour ago: the slams of her tiny fists against that ugly barrier; her instinctual rage against it—the state-made blockade raised under the rubric of security, her hot tears.

They haunt me.

November 1994

"On tilt" by state design

Harry Washington* shrieks out of an internal orgy of psychic pain: "*Niggers!!* Keep my family's name outcha *mouf!* Ya *freaks!* Ya *filth!* Ya racist *garbage! All* my family believe in God! Keep your twisted Satanic filth to Y'all*self!* Keep my family's name outch'all nasty *mouf!!*"

I have stopped the reflexive glance down in front of Harry's cell. For now, as in all the times in the past, I know no one is out near his ground-level cell—I know Harry is in a mouth-foaming rage because of the ceaseless noises echoing within the chambers of his tortured mind. For Harry and I are among the growing numbers of Pennsylvanians on death row, and Harry, because of mind-snapping isolation, a bitterly rac-

---

* Not his real name, although quotes and historical facts are true.

ist environment, and the ironies, the auguries of fate, has begun the slide from depression, through deterioration, to dementia.

While we both share the deadening effects of isolation, and an environment straight out of the redneck boondocks, Harry, like so many others, has slipped. Many of his tormenters here (both real and imagined) have named him "Nut" and describe him as "on tilt." Perhaps the cruel twists of fate popped his cork—who can say? A young black man, once a correctional officer, now a death row convict. Once he wore the keys, now he hears the keys, in an agonizing wait for death. The conditions of most of America's death rows create Harry Washingtons by the score.

Mix in solitary confinement, around-the-clock lock-in, no-contact visits, no prison jobs, no educational programs by which to grow, psychiatric "treatment" facilities designed only to drug you into a coma; ladle in hostile, overtly racist prison guards and staff; add the weight of the falling away of family ties, and you have all the fixings for a stressful psychic stew designed to deteriorate, to erode one's humanity—designed, that is, by the state, with full knowledge of its effects.

Nearly a century ago, a Colorado man was sentenced to death for killing his wife. On his arrival at Colorado State Penitentiary, James Medley was placed in solitary. Medley promptly brought an original writ of habeas corpus in the U.S. Supreme Court, which in 1890 consisted of six Republicans and three Democrats. In the case, *In Re Medley* 134 U.S. 160 (1890), the Court reached back to old English law, to the early 1700s of King George II, to conclude that solitary confinement was "an additional punishment of the most important and painful character" and, as applied to Medley, unconstitutional.

Fast-forward nearly a century, to 1986, to the infamous federal court decision of *Peterkin v. Jeffes*,* where Pennsylvania death row inmates sought to have solitary confinement declared unconstitutional, and one hears a judge deny relief, saying, in the immortal words of now chief justice Rehnquist, "Nobody promised them a rose garden,"† that is, solitary is okay.

---

* *Peterkin v. Jeffes* 661 F Supp. 895 (E. D. Pa. 1987) or 885 F.2d 1021 (3rd Cir. 1988).

† *Atiyeh v. Capps* 449 U.S. 1312, 66 L.Ed.2d 785.

The notion that human progress is marked by "an evolving standard of decency,"* from the less civilized to the more civilized, from the more restrictive to the less restrictive, from tyranny to expanding freedom, dies a quick death on the rocks of today's Rehnquistian courts. Indeed, what other court could make the Republican-controlled, Southern-Harlan-Fuller Court of the 1890s seem positively radical by comparison?

Harry continues his howlings and mindless mutterings of rage at no one in particular.

June 1989

---

* Full quotation is "evolving standards of decency that mark the progress of a maturing society" *Trop v. Dulles* 356 U.S. S.Ct., 86 101, 78 S.Ct. 590, 598, 2. L.Ed.2d. 630 (1958).

On death row:
fade to black

It is about time the Court faced the fact that the white people in the South don't like the colored people.

—*William H. Rehnquist, law clerk, 1953**

A light-skinned native of Lenape lineage sidles up to a fellow prisoner in a nearby steel cage for a bit of small talk.

"Damn, man," the Indian youth exclaims in his northeastern Pennsylvania nasal twang, "I been here too damn long."

"Why you say dat, Runnin' Bear?"

"Well cuz I caught myself sayin' 'poh-leece' insteada 'puh-leese,' [police] and 'fo' insteada 'four.' "

---

* Adler, Renata; *The New Republic*; "The Bork-Rehnquist Poison," Sept., 14-21, 1987, p. 45.

32

The two men yuk it up. Gallows humor.

Bear, for the first time in his life, lives in a predominantly black community, albeit an artificial, warped one, for it is bereft of the laughter of women or the bawling of babes.

Only men "live" here. Mostly young black men.

Welcome to Huntingdon's death row, one of three in Pennsylvania. The denizens of death row are black as molasses, and the staff are white bread.

Long-termers on the row, those here since 1984, recall a small but seemingly significant event that took place back then. Maintenance and construction staff, forced by a state court order and state statute to provide men with a minimum of two hours daily outside exercise, rather than the customary fifteen minutes every other day, erected a number of steel, cyclone-fenced boxes, which strikingly resemble dog runs or pet pens. Although staff assured inmates that the pens would be used only for disciplinary cases, the construction ended and the assurances were put to the test. The first day after completion of the cages, death cases, all free of any disciplinary infractions, were marched out to the pens for daily exercise outdoors. Only when the cages were full did full recognition dawn that all the caged men were African.

Where were the white cons of death row?

A few moments of silent observation proved the obvious. The death row block offered direct access to two yards: one composed of cages, the other "free" space, water fountains, full-court basketball spaces and hoops, and an area for running. The cages were for the blacks on death row. The open yards were for the whites on the row. The blacks, due to racist insensitivity and sheer hatred, were condemned to awaiting death in indignity. The event provided an excellent view, in microcosm, of the mentality of the criminal system of injustice, suffused by the toxin of racism.

The notes of a youthful law clerk of 1953 are the ruling opinions of America's highest court of today. The clerk of yesteryear is today's chief justice, and the word *South* can be juxtaposed with *North*, *West*, *East*, or even *Court*, with equal applicability. A people who once looked to the Court for enlightened protection now face only hostility. Nowhere is that clearer than in capital cases before the Court, for at the heart of this country's death penalty scheme is the crucible of race.

Who would dare argue otherwise after examining the pivotal case *McCleskey v. Kemp* (1987), where the Court took a delicate moonwalk backward, away from a mountain of awesome evidence that showed incontrovertibly that (1) defendants charged with killing white victims in Georgia are 4.3 times as likely to be sentenced to death as defendants charged with killing blacks; (2) race [of the victim] determines whether a death penalty is returned; (3) nearly six of every eleven defendants convicted of killing whites would not have gotten the death penalty had their victims been black; (4) twenty of every thirty-four black defendants would not have received the death penalty had their victims been black; and (5) cases involving black defendants and white victims are more likely to result in a death sentence than cases featuring any other racial combination of defendant and victim. McCleskey's claims, wrote the Court's centrist, Justice Powell, cannot prevail, because "taken to its logical conclusion, McCleskey throws into serious question the principles that underlie our entire criminal justice system."*

Put quite another way, the *McCleskey* Court denied relief, while accepting as valid his data proving the above five statements, not because his studies or their conclusions were untrue but because of the impact such findings would have on other cases. Welcome to the Great March Backward.

McCleskey, of course, was not alone. At base, *McCleskey* revealed a system of demonstrable, documented imbalance, where race of victim and race of defendant determined whether one would live or die. This, the Court said, was perfectly constitutional.

Robert A. Burt, a Yale Law scholar, has examined the implications of *McCleskey* in light of the 1986 case *Lockhart v. McCree*, where the Court similarly rejected the argument that a death-qualified, pro-prosecution, pro-capital punish-

---

* *McCleskey v. Kemp* 481 U.S. 279 (1987); *Lockhart v. McCree* U.S. Ark., 106 S. Ct., 1758 90 L.Ed. 137.

ment jury* offends the fundamental constitutional command for a fair, impartial jury. Professor Burt notes:

> When we add this finding [i.e., that *Lockhart* juries tend to be white and male because blacks and women are generally anti–death penalty and are, thus, excluded] to the evidence gathered in *McCleskey*, that capital juries impose the death penalty with disproportionate frequency on blacks who murder whites and infrequently in response to any murders of blacks, a grim portrait of the American Criminal Justice system emerges. This portrait shows that law enforcement in the most serious and publicly visible cases is entrusted predominantly to groups of white men who value white lives more than blacks; and thus they take special vengeance on blacks who murder whites and are much less concerned about the murder of blacks. Indeed, its low valuation of blacks coupled with its special arousal when blacks murder whites suggests

---

* Definition of *death-qualified jury*: in order to be seated a jury must be able to impose penalties prescribed by the law, such as the death penalty, therefore any person not able to vote for the death penalty can not sit on a jury in a capital case. Hence, these juries are pro-prosecution, pro-conviction, pro–death penalty.

a law enforcement regime that acts as if our society were gripped by fears about, and prepared to take preemptive strikes against, an explosion of race warfare.*

As of 7/25/88, the state court administrator's office recorded 107 people on Pennsylvania's death row, and, of that total, 50 from Philadelphia alone. Of that 50, 40 were of African blood, with 7 whites and 3 Hispanics. Statewide, blacks, only 9 percent of the population, emerge as a clear majority on Pennsylvania's death row.

Nationally, the picture is equally bleak, as Africans, just over 11 percent of the nation's total, grow into 40 percent of America's national death row. More often than not, capital punishment in America carries a black, brown, or red face.

From daybreak to dusk, black voices resound in exchanges of daily dramas that mark time in the dead zone; the latest on a lawyer; the latest on a lover; tidbits of thought bouncing off bars of

---

* Burt, Robert A., *Disorder in the Court: The Death Penalty and the Constitution*; 85 Mich. L. Rev. 1798 (Aug. 1987). A Yale Law scholar examined the implications of McCleskey in light of the 1986 case *Lockhart v. McCree* U.S. Ark., 106 S.Ct., 1758 90 L.Ed. 137.

steel and walls of stone, relentlessly, in the wait for death.

Echoes of *Dred Scott* ring in today's *McCleskey* opinion, again noting the paucity of rights held by Africans in the land of the free, who "had for more than a century before been regarded as beings of an inferior order, and altogether unfit to associate with the white race, either in social or political relations; and so far inferior, that they had no rights which the white man was bound to respect."*

Chief Justice Taney sits again, reincarnate, on the Rehnquist Court of the Modern Age. Taney's Court, in *Scott*, left intact the power of the slaver by denying constitutional rights to Africans, even those born in the United States. Rehnquist's Court, in *McCleskey*, leaves intact the power of the state to further cheapen black life.

One hundred and thirty-three years after *Scott*, and still unequal in life, as in death.

April 1990

---

* *Dred Scott v. Sanford* 19 U.S. (How.) 393, 407, 15 L.Ed. 691 (1857); quoted verbatim.

From an echo in darkness, a step into light

"Pssst! Pssst!! Yo, Mu! Mu! You up?" asks the Italian-Cherokee tier runner, his accent betraying his South Philly roots. Stirring from the mattress, I trudge to the cell door, look down to where Mike stands, and glower at his bright face.

"What's up, man?" I grumble at sleep's interruption.

"You ready for this?" Mike asks rhetorically, his face ablaze with a smile.

"Man, what's up?" I demand, a bit peeved at the wordplay.

"Jay Smith?? He's going home!" Mike announces, and a heartfelt sense of happiness at another man's good fortune lifts my mood instantly.

"No shit, Mike?"

40

"Swear to God, Mu—he's packin' his gear right now. Sez he gotta order from the Supreme Court throwin' out his conviction! Ain't that somethin'?"

"Yeah, Mike. That's somethin' wonderful! Long live *John Africa*! That's good news, man!"

Jay Smith, a common, Anglo-Saxon, everyday American name, belonged to an old, quiet, gray-haired, professional white dude who, until recently, was among 149 souls on Pennsylvania's death row after his conviction for three killings that sparked national attention, several books, and a television movie.* Prosecutors, police, and the press painted him as an archdemon, a twisted sadist, a triple killer, and an all-around not-so-nice guy, light-years from the Lower Merion school principal and army reservist his neighbors and students knew.

Having read a news article depicting him as cold and evil with "goatlike" gray eyes, I half expected when I met him to see him bounding around on two cloven hooves. But, on appeal, it appeared as if the real animals (skunks) sent him

---

* *Commonwealth of Pennsylvania v. Jay Smith* 532 Pa. 177; 615 A.2d 321 (1992).

to death row, for the Supreme Court reversed his conviction, citing prosecutorial misconduct, and his lawyer steadily uncovered lying cops, hidden evidence, and secret deals between investigators and a Hollywood novelist for inside info on the case. His prosecutor, who rose to national office on his case, fell just as swiftly when arrested and convicted on cocaine-related charges.

On Friday, September 18, 1992, at midday, the word came to Smith that his case was over; the prosecution discharged; the defendant free to go. Encaged in Pennsylvania hellholes and on death row since 1979, Jay Smith packed his meager possessions, sent a few bye-byes around, shook off the ashes of twelve years, and walked away, stepping back into life. All the books, the multimillion-dollar movies of the week, and the damning news articles paled beside the reality of one man, walking from the stagnant cesspool of prison into freedom.

When one reporter asked him about his plans, he replied, "I dunno. I've been fighting so long for this that I hadn't planned for anything beyond. I'm sixty-four—maybe in a year I can collect social security?" But what "security" exists in a system that plotted, lied, connived, and hid evidence to destroy one man's life, that took twelve years from his life, his profession, his family?

September 1992

Nightraiders meet rage

A single spark can start a prairie fire.

—*Mao Ze-dong*

Prisons are repositories of rage, islands of socially acceptable hatreds, where worlds collide like subatomic particles seeking psychic release. Like Chairman Mao's proverbial spark, it takes little to start the blazes banked within repressive breasts.

I thought of that spark one morning recently when I heard an eruption of violence that hit Huntingdon's B block, snatching the writer from the false escape of dreams.

A white man's rural twang spat out a rhetorical question: "Oh! You like hurtin' people, huh?" Punches, grunts, thuds, and crunches echoed up the steel tiers, awakening the groggy into sudden alertness.

"Getta fuck offa that man!"

"Leave that man alone, you fat, racist pussy!"

A quiet morning on B block was shattered, as much by the yells of fearful rage as by the blams of baton on flesh and bone. Predictably, the beating and taunts continued, until the man was thrown into a locked shower and was able to call up to others also locked in and inform them of what had transpired.

"Who is it, man?" "What's yo name, dude?"

"Tim . . ."

"Tim Forrest," he answered, sounding hyped but guarded.

"What happened, Timmy?"

"They rolled on me, man, for fighting that dude, Weaverling."

Timmy?

The voice was familiar, because he recently worked over on B block as a tier runner for several months, lugging food trays and handling other menial block-maintenance chores, working around death row and disciplinary prisoners. I liked the guy—thirtyish, slight of build, with an outgoing personality—despite our strong political differences.

"You can't fight these people, Mu," Tim

45

opined, adding "You can't beat the system." I sniffed in strong disapproval, but he ignored my argument. So we rapped music, a common love, and I enjoyed his melodious tenor crooning.

Timmy? Fighting a guard? Fighting a slew of guards?

By Friday, the rumor spread of Tim's treatment at B block, and following midday Jumu'ah* services, more than fifty men converged on the prison's center to demand an end to the brutal beatings of cuffed men. Caught by surprise, ranking security officers assured the angry black throng that no such beatings would occur, and urged dispersal. By nightfall, an uneasy quiet loomed over the central Pennsylvania prison. Come Saturday morning, lockdown was launched—no movement, no jobs, no recreation, no trays served—a regimen of utter restriction.

Overnight, Pennsylvania's most repressive jail became Pennsylvania's largest "hole."

The weekend passed in lockdown, and on Monday, when a mournful siren sounded, there

---

* *Jumu'ah*: Congregational Islamic prayers performed on Fridays beginning after the sun passes its zenith.

was confusion, disbelief, and then a smattering of applause as some assumed jailbreak, which usually precedes the sounding of the township-wide alarm.

The foghorn cries faded, then cried again, then faded, and then cried anew. Confusion overtook jubilation, and the applause faded to embarrassed silence.

Walkie-talkies snapped to life, and the ring of keys sounded throughout the jail, as all three shifts converged en masse at dusk. Armed, armored squads went from cell to cell, pulling, cuffing, punching, bludgeoning, kicking, brutalizing naked prisoners. Men were handcuffed, seized, dragged outside, and thrown into cages, naked, beaten, and bloodied. Huntingdon's revenge for Friday's loss of face rivaled Dixie slavocracy for its premeditated racist raids.

Men, naked, unarmed, awakened from deep sleep, fought back against the rural mob, bravely, perhaps none too wisely. By Tuesday morning, unofficial reports put the injured at twenty-seven staff, nineteen inmates, with A block in shambles, as lockdown continued. By Wednesday, the cages were being hosed down, traces of blood washed into drains to feed the Juniata River, washed away.

As of this writing, the lockdown—no showers, no jobs, no movement, no recreation—continues, as Huntingdon prison becomes Huntingdon hole. One participant in the bloody fracas, asked to tell what happened, answered, "It's just like Mao said, man—'One spark can start a prairie fire'!"

October 1989

Actin' like life's a ball game

When I hear politicians bellow about "getting tough on crime" and barking out "three strikes, you're out" rhetoric, several images come to mind. I think of how quickly the tune changes when the politician is on the receiving end of some of that so-called toughness, after having fallen from grace.

I am reminded of a powerful state appellate judge who, once caught in an intricate, bizarre web of criminal conduct, changed his longstanding opinion regarding the efficacy of the insanity defense, an option he once ridiculed. It revealed in a flash how illusory and transitory power and status can be, and how we are all, after all, human.

I also think of a young man I met in prison who was one of the first wave of people imprisoned back in the 1970s under new, tougher youth certification statutes that allowed teenagers to be sentenced as adults. The man, whom I'll call Rabbani, was a tall, husky fifteen-year-old when he was arrested in southeastern Pennsylvania for armed robbery. The prosecutor moved that he be judicially certified as an adult, and the Court agreed. Tried as an adult, Rabbani was convicted of all charges and sentenced to fifteen to thirty years in prison, for an alleged robbery with a CO_2 air pistol.

His first six or seven years in this man-made hell found him constantly locked in battles with guards, and he logged more years in the "hole" than he did in general population status. He grew into manhood in shackles, and every time I saw him he seemed bigger in size but more bitter in spirit.

When we took the time to converse, I was always struck by the innate brilliance of the young man—a brilliance immersed in bitterness, a bitterness so acidic that it seemed capable of dissolving steel. For almost fifteen years this brilliance had been caged in steel; for almost two of these years he tried, largely in vain, to get a judge to reconsider his case, but the one-line, two-word denials—"appeal denied"—only served to deepen his profound cynicism.

For those critical years in the life of a male, from age fifteen to thirty, which mark the transition from boy to man, Rabbani was entombed in a juridical, psychic, temporal box branded with the false promise "corrections." Like tens of thousands of his generation, his time in hell equipped him with no skills of value to either himself or his community. He has been "corrected" in precisely the same way that hundreds of thousands of others have been, that is to say, warehoused in a vat that sears the very soul.

He has never held a woman as a mate or lover; he has never held a newborn in his palm, its heart athump with new life; he hasn't seen the sun rise, nor the moon glow, in almost fifteen years—for a robbery, "armed" with a pellet gun, at fifteen years old.

When I hear easy, catchy, mindless slogans like "three strikes, you're out," I think of men like Rabbani who had *one* strike (if not one foul) and are, for all intents and purposes, already outside of any game worth playing.

March 1994

Legal outlaws: Bobby's battle for justice

The name Bobby Brightwell was not a new one. In my mind's eye, he stood garbed in clearest memory: short, stocky, 230 pounds, sitting easily on a well-muscled, superbly conditioned frame, with an elfish, perpetual grin on his face that gave birth to belly laughs from a face turned reddish brown by midsummer. Memory proved a poor match for the description given of the Bobby Brightwell seen just days ago on a witness stand in a Cumberland County courthouse: pale, listless, sickly, shrunken to nearly 150 pounds, a body bent on atrophy. "He looked like an old man," said one spectator. What could cause such a dramatic deterioration in just three years? Brightwell, barely forty, was not just a witness but the defendant in his own prison assault trial, stemming from incidents that occurred in April 1992, in Rockview prison, central Pennsylvania.

The story that Bobby told from the witness stand was a harrowing revelation of official barbarity, a reflection of what happens daily in the state-constructed shadows called prisons across America. Brightwell had a prison history of being a complainer—one who files institutional complaints against staff members who violate their own rules—and thus had earned the enmity of prison staffers.

On April 10, 1992, shortly before noon, he was returning from the prison exercise yard while handcuffed, escorted by four armed (with batons) guards. He was searched repeatedly, and after the fourth such search he rightly inquired why. He was ordered to face the wall, and as he did so, he was punched in the back of the head and the neck, called "nigger," and warned to "mind your goddamn business!" A lieutenant grabbed a baton and, using its tip like a dagger, jabbed Brightwell forcefully and repeatedly in his belly, knocking the wind out of the handcuffed captive. On his return to his cell, the sergeant intentionally slammed the metal cell gate into him, and when he made his way to the toilet, Brightwell vomited, and later urinated and defecated blood. Shortly thereafter, he was taken to the prison's psychiatric observation unit, a strip cell with nothing—no toilet (a hole in the floor), no sheets, nothing except a mattress drenched in urine.

It wasn't until April 13, three days later, that he saw a doctor, who briefly prescribed a liquid diet, but even now Bobby has difficulty keeping his food down. On April 21, 1992, per order of prison deputies, Bobby was ordered moved from the strip cell, and returned to the restricted housing unit (RHU), site of the initial assault, despite his pleas and clear fears of retaliation. Such pleas fell on deaf ears, and on his brief return he was literally thrown into a cell with a nonfunctional light and beaten again, by approximately ten guards, who knocked his glasses off with punches, pulled his arms, choked him, and pummeled him so that, as he told the court, "I felt punches and pain everywhere."

Knocked to the steel bunk, he yelled in a mad fit of pain, "Why don't you just break 'em off?" as his legs were pulled savagely apart and sadistically twisted. He lay, twisted, cuffed, and shackled to a leather restraint, for over five hours, denied medical treatment and vomiting, before being returned to DW.

In early September 1992, on trial under charges of assault by life prisoner, a common pleas jury found him not guilty, acquitting him of all charges.

A trial observer said that when the verdict was returned, Brightwell didn't even smile. His mind probably was taken up with a picture of his tormentors, the guards, the well-paid civil servants, who stole all but his very life and who have never been charged with anything.

September 1992

Manny's attempted murder

At first glance the guy looks like a black fire-plug. Short, coffee-black, with a clean-shaven, glistening dome, Manny resembles a miniversion of boxing great Jack Johnson. An ex-boxer of champion status himself, Manny moves with well-muscled agility as if always in a ring. Bigger prisoners regard him with a wary respect. Lately, though, his moves have been a little less than agile, a trifle forced.

Manny's recent history seems plucked from the pages of a Robert Ludlum spy-murder mystery, but it is no tale—it is chillingly, utterly true.

A lifelong epileptic, Manny's life has revolved around the daily ingestion of the anticonvulsant Dilantin with the sedative phenobarbital. His last ten years or so were virtually seizure-free, until he arrived at Huntingdon and came under the "care" of its medical staff.

After an apparent setup and serious altercation with a white inmate, resulting in his assailant's hospitalization, Manny was sent to the D.C. (disciplinary custody) max unit, a walled "prison within a prison."

There, the mystery.

There, the attempted murder.

No attack on a handcuffed inmate, the joint's usual M.O. Tools change with the times, it seems.

While in the "max," Manny experienced a series of seizures, powerful enough to leave him locked in a deep coma.

"What the fuck is goin' on?" he asked himself. He paid extra-close attention to his food. He waited. He watched. He fasted. Still, the seizures came, in waves of increasing frequency and mind-numbing power. Why, he wondered? Why now? He noticed new medications being administered—new colors, new quantities—and asked questions: "What's this?" The answers, provided by the same persons who gave medication, the guards, were easy, breezy lies: "Aw, nothin'—a new kinda Dilantin, the nurse sez—wancher medication?"

The more he took, the worse he got; the more

57

powerful the seizures, the deeper the comas. He stopped. He filed complaints; he demanded and obtained outside medical care. At Altoona's hospital, Manny got his answers.

In addition to his Dilantin/phenobarbital regimen, someone had slipped in the drugs Loxitane, Artane, and Haldol (haloperidol). The mixture was like a chemical cannonball, wreaking havoc on his vision, his balance, and, most ominously, his liver.

When an internist began to conduct a microbiopsy on his liver, and then halted, refused to go further, and sewed him back up, Manny's instincts took over. Something was very wrong. The surgeon at Altoona told him there was a glasslike sheath over his liver, and ultrasound showed that it was swollen and distended. The Haldol, according to the authoritative *Physician's Desk Reference*, was contraindicated to use with anticonvulsants (such as Dilantin) because it "lowers the convulsive threshold"; in a nutshell, it *causes* seizure!

In dizzying internal pain, Manny continues his battles against the prison medical bureaucracy that brought him from championship form to the brink of death.

That he lives is itself a miracle.

That he fights is by power of will.

That the culprits, those who prescribed this toxic chemical cocktail, still lay hidden is an indictment against a racist system of corruption, masquerading as corrections.

Meanwhile, he waits, he fights, he strengthens himself.

April 1989

A toxic shock

A prisoner, sodden with the haze of sleep, makes his morning stagger to the commode, does his daily do, punches in the cold-water button, and, cupping, tries to rinse grogginess out of heavy eyelids. In a flash, he is awake with clarity, and alarm, but it is not the cold water's doing. His nose rebels. His lips wrinkle into a curl. Up and down the block, voices rise in anger.

"Hey, man—you smell that water?!?"

"What the fuck?!"

"Hey, dude, this shit smell like gasoline!"

Gagging and spitting are heard, and a day begins at Huntingdon gulag in central Pennsylvania.

The thick, stinging smell roams the block, cutting through steel and brick, as if, by its leaden ubiquity, only it is free of containment. "Water up! Water up!" chants fill the morning

air, ricocheting like verbal bullets, echoing, ca-
reening from cell to cell.

About an hour later, guards tour the block,
issuing warnings: "Don't drink the water. We'll
be bringing some by. Don't drink the water. . . ."
By midday the promise is fulfilled, and water
tanked in by the National Guard begins to wash
the nasty edge off more than two thousand
thirsts. Water, I ruminate. How sweet. How we
take this stuff for granted. It appears this water
problem is more than prisonwide; civilian communities, sharing the same water source, are also
affected.

A phrase from legendary MOVE founder *John
Africa* flies to mind, about the system: "Taking
our water, familiar and clean, and turning it into
a potion that's poison" (from *The Judge's Letter*,
by *John Africa*). By nightfall, a memo from the
warden announces that "an oil based substance
has washed its way into institutional springs, due
to heavy rains." (No word on what the substance
is.) Also, a warning: do not drink the water. By
midday following, another memo announces
that the Pennsylvania Department of Environ-
mental Resources has pronounced the water
"perfectly safe to drink." In one day!

61

The heavy gaseous odor still lingers, and a dark oily ring stains cups. It makes me wonder about a saying my wife and I share, that bars and steel can't stop the power of love. The dark side of that also is true: bars, steel, and court orders can't stop the seepage of pollution that afflicts both the caged and the "free." Despite the legal illusions erected by the system to divide and separate life, we the caged share air, water, and hope with you, the not-yet-caged. We share your same breath. As *John Africa* teaches, "All life is connected."

It was, for me, a jarring revelation. For an instant it took me beyond the bars, and over the walls, to Love Canal, New York; to Times Beach; and to toxic dumps known and unknown, which sit like silent springs of death.

I think of white, well-fed families who survive and thrive off houses of pain like this, in rural enclaves across the country, under the illusion of otherness. How many housewives in the surrounding township met sunrise this morning with sleep in their eyes, filled the pot with water for coffee, caught a whiff of gasoline rising from the cup, and gagged?

The earth is but one great ball. The borders, the barriers, the cages, the cells, the prisons of our lives, all originate in the false imagination of the minds of men.

May 1989

Spirit death

Much has been written and much has been said about "life" within prison. Some write of the glaring incidents of violence that occur, certain that such subjects will grab the attention of the reader. Others write and play down the violence, lest the reader jettison those dark visions, so distant from his or her experience, as simply beyond belief. As ever, the truth oscillates somewhere in between.

That prisons are hotbeds of violence is undeniable, but overt expressions of violence are rarely daily ones. The most profound horror of prisons lives in the day-to-day banal occurrences that turn days into months, and months into years, and years into decades. Prison is a second-by-second assault on the soul, a day-to-day degradation of the self, an oppressive steel and brick umbrella that transforms seconds into hours and hours into days. While a person is locked away in distant netherworlds, time seems to stand still; but it doesn't, of course. Children left outside grow into adulthood, often having children of their own. Once loving relationships wither into yesterday's dust. Relatives die, their loss mourned in silent loneliness. Times, temperaments, mores change, and the caged move to outdated rhythms.

Encased within a psychic cocoon of negativity, the bad get worse and feed on evil's offal. Those who are harmed become further damaged, and the merely warped are twisted. Empty unproductive hours morph into years of nothingness. This is the furrowed face of "corrections" in this age, where none are corrected, where none emerge better than when they came in. This is the face of "correction," which outlaws education among those who have an estimated 60 percent illiteracy rate.

The mind-numbing, soul-killing savage sameness that makes each day an echo of the day before, with neither thought nor hope of growth, makes prison the abode of spirit death that it is for over a million men and women now held in U.S. hellholes. What societal interest is served by prisoners who remain illiterate? What social benefit is there in ignorance? How are people corrected while imprisoned if their education is outlawed? Who profits (other than the prison establishment itself) from stupid prisoners?

November 1994

A return to death

One would think a person on death row would be used to bad news.

Not so.

No one gets used to it.

Two men regard each other warily, as they converse within a steel cage, their only opportunity in a twenty-four-hour day to feel a ray of sunshine or breathe air relatively fresh (considering the rich aroma of cowshit that rides languorously on the spring breeze). Both men have recently been denied relief by the state's highest court, in their continuing quest for escape from death, and freedom.

"Damn, Chuck—I'm sorry you got slimed, man. The only reason they did that foul stuff is cuza me."

"Hey, Mu, you ain't got nothin' to be sorry for, man. You didn't do it, they did."

"Yeah, man, but when I read the opinion, all it said was my case! I had to keep lookin' at the caption to be sure it wasn't '*Commonwealth v. Abu-Jamal*',* instead of '*Commonwealth v. Beasley*'!† Didn't you think so, man, when you read that damn opinion?"

"*What* damn opinion?"

"Whatchu mean, Chuck?"

"I mean, I ain't read no opinion."

"So, how'd you find out you got shot down?"

"Same way I thought *you* found out—I read it ina newspaper."

"Yo, Chuck, you sayin' you ain't heard from your lawyer?"

"Sheeeeeit, Mu, I ain't heard from my lawyer since February 1988, when I first gotta death sentence flipped."

"Getta hell outta here!"

"Man, don't you think I would if I could?"

The men laugh at the witty line, but it is not a belly laugh. Beasley's mouth is in a wide smile, but his eyes do not laugh, for there is little reason

---

* *Commonwealth v. Abu-Jamal* 521 Pa. 188, 555 A.2d 846 (1989).
† *Commonwealth v. Beasley* 524 Pa. 34, 568 A.2d 1235 (1990).

for joy. And if eyes are indeed mirrors of the soul, then they reflect an infinite sadness.

I look away, afraid of what mine might reflect.

Both Beasley and I have shared enough for one lifetime: The same judge. The same prosecutor. The same entreaty to the jury that they are "not being asked to kill anybody," for the defendant "has appeals after appeals after appeals, and there might be a reversal or whatever." In February 1988, Pennsylvania's intermediate appeals court, the state superior court, reviewed that argument to the jury in *Beasley* and pronounced it improper, and misleading, holding that the death penalty could not stand.

Two years later, in late January, the Pennsylvania Supreme Court reversed the superior court order, thus reinstating the death sentence. (The same day my petition for reargument was denied.) What a fact to discover from a week-old newspaper!

To do so, the state's highest court, in an exercise of legal legerdemain, mistakenly cited sections of the argument made to my jury, in the guilt/innocence phase, to justify arguments made in the sentencing phase of *Beasley*, in violation of its own prior precedent in *Commonwealth v. Baker*,* and rulings of the U.S. Supreme Court in *Caldwell v. Mississippi*† (1985).

Pennsylvania's superior court, citing *Caldwell/ Baker* error, lifted Beasley's death sentence; the Pennsylvania's Supreme Court, citing *Abu-Jamal*, gave it back to him, two years later.

The two men play a few lackluster games of cage/handball, but their hearts are not in it. Their minds are miles away, on loved ones choking in silent pain, on legal strategies for tomorrow, on a system based on law that changes like the fickle central Pennsylvania weather.

April 1990

---

* *Commonwealth v. Baker* 511 Pa. 1, 511 A.2d 777 (1986).
† *Caldwell v. Mississippi* 472 U.S. 320 (1985).

Days of pain—
night of death

The gray-haired tier runner brought the morning coffee, and the latest news—a shocker.

"Remember that dude Woolfolk, Mu?"

"Yeah, what about 'im?"

"He hung up last nite."

"Gitta hell outta here, man! You jokin'?"

"No joke, man. He's dead. They carried him out last nite."

My mind flipped to a quiet night's sleep, with no awareness of the tragedy unfolding several cells away from mine, a night of one man's anguish, ended by a knotted sheet.

Craig Woolfolk, about forty-one, manic as hell—his whining, scratchy whiskey voice, and nonstop chatter, a source of anger to many—has finally stopped.

Woolfolk—I loved the name, but didn't quite care for the man. The name Woolfolk seemed one so apt for black folk; the man was a manic chatterbox, and his voice stole many nights of rest. I thought of his unexpected, presumed suicide, and thought of many others, Pipehead just weeks ago, that have sought death's relief. It made me think of a brief written by MOVE martyr and naturalist minister Frank Africa, in the infamous case *Africa v. Commonwealth of Pennsylvania* (1981),* where MOVE sought its religious diet.

Holding, as expected, for the state and against the prisoner, the court rejected relief, but the point was made. In naturalist minister Frank's brief, he explains, with startling oratory, the contradiction between the state's denial of health and its diet of death:

Our Principle, given to us through the generosity of Our Teacher [*John Africa*], cuts through the bitterness of jealousy, fills in the emptiness that causes this hatred, and generates respect and trust where

---

* *Africa v. Commonwealth of Pennsylvania*, 662 F.2d 1025 (3rd Cir. 1981); Third circuit held that MOVE was not entitled to religious protection.

jealousy once was. And this is proven at the prisons where our diet is already established, for we are *widely* respected because we are direction *giving* to all those that suffer the deprivation that this system practices. . . . Anytime this system's prisons supply a steady diet of cigarettes that deprive folks of their health, provides a diet of junk food that deprives folks of their teeth, perpetuates a diet of perversion that deprives folks of their sex, stipulates a diet of birth control that deprives folks of their fertility, promotes a diet of drug ridden foods and mind torturing medications that deprives folks of their *very sanity*, and questions the relevance of *our* diet, while leaving this insanity unquestioned, this backwards analysis needs to be closely examined, for our diet is unquestionably innocent, but this disorder is as questionable as the chaotic reference it was derived from. This is why it is also foolish to deny us our diet for fear of prisoners making wine, this is a blatant insult, because it is the prisons, this system that indulges and flaunts this distortion wherever it touches, and *not* MOVE, *John Africa* has made us clean people, wise people, made us godly people. . . . It is ridiculous for this system's prisons to express concern about wine making, and schizophrenically pump thorazine, booze people with

73

slow juice, phenobarbitals, drunken folks bodies with all manner of *devastating*, emotion wrecking chemicals, robbing their soberness with a weapon of barbiturates, intoxicating folks with up drugs and down drugs and all in between, and *leaving* them drunk and staggering with hopelessness that *drives* them to *collapse* in the clutches of suicide in attempt to escape this diabolical treachery, causing them to hang themselves in seek of relief, pushing them to slit their wrists, gash their throats, crack their skulls in desperation to try and alleviate the pain that this system inflicts, forcing folks to the edge of insanity and leaving them no choice but to jump to their death. . . . We have seen this tragedy time and again, stretchers carting the victims of this atrocity murdered by this intruder that practices torment.

Question: Why do they still call it "corrections"?

January 1990

Relatives decry
"camp hell"

> The degree of civilization in a society can be judged by
> entering the prisons.
>
> —*Fyodor Dostoyevsky*, The House of the Dead

The infamous Camp Hill prison, in midstate
Pennsylvania, site of a raging two-day fiery riot,
is now becoming more notorious, but for its
staff, not its inmates. As after the dreaded Attica
rebellion, prisoners faced a postriot round of
repression that bordered on the barbaric.* The
Harrisburg Sunday Patriot-News reports that a
campaign of torture, theft, terror, and degrada-

---

* "Attica rebellion: 43 inmates and hostages lay dead after the
4-day rebellion at New York State's Attica Correctional Facility in
September 1971. Many more were wounded." The official report
of the New York State Special Commission on Attica. Bantam
Books.

tion greeted prisoners in the aftermath of riotous rage.

Initially, inmates were handcuffed and shackled to other inmates, and held for three days this way, outside, in the prison yard. This came to an end only after the Pennsylvania chapter of the American Civil Liberties Union (ACLU) stepped in and, petitioning before a U.S. district judge, was granted a temporary restraining order barring the medieval practice, but not before "correctional" officials took advantage of the practice to further humiliate prisoners at the medium-security facility.

As one inmate wrote: "When you want to go to the toilet . . . they wanted the person standing to [wipe] the other inmate . . . since he couldn't do it himself because we were all handcuffed. When the inmate wouldn't do it, he got hit with clubs and both of them had to lie down in the middle of the basketball court, face down" (*Harrisburg Sunday Patriot-News*, November 26, 1989). The central Pennsylvania paper reported that more than a dozen letters were received from prisoners, all of whom sought anonymity for fear of reprisal. Personal inmate property was destroyed willy-nilly, except for jewelry, which was simply stolen by staffers, as one prisoner noted: "I saw a guard with my wedding band on his pinkie." Needless to say, state prison spokesmen simply claimed to be investigating the charges, one being that a guard stuck a lit cigarette into a man's ear, for "fun."

Lois Williamson, the fiery Philadelphia grandmother who heads the regional chapter of Citizens United for the Rehabilitation of Errants (CURE), told reporters that inmates who tell of mistreatment are brutally punished. A letter home, which results in a relative calling up the prison, has brought beatings to several prisoners, the prison reformer related. Incidentally, Williamson was fired from the volunteer staff of the crusty Pennsylvania Prison Society in late 1988 for daring to publicly criticize the Pennsylvania Department of Corrections for its record of brutality, unresponsiveness, and severe overcrowdedness, during a nationally televised interview.

The Pennsylvania Prison Society, in revoking her official visiting status, claimed that the outspoken activist hampered the agency's credibility with prison administrators. Now, with news reports circulating worldwide about "Camp Hell," it is Mrs. Williamson's criticisms that seem quite credible, and inmates and relatives see the society as unresponsive, and incestuously close to an agency of government that has neither the will nor the wherewithal to detain people without making them irrevocably worse.

Guards who steal, who brutalize, who intentionally humiliate people, in the name of the people, are a mockery of the term "correctional officer." A department of government that tolerates, ignores, conveniently overlooks such acts of state criminality, while sanctioning prisoners for the most trivial of alleged transgressions, is not worthy of the name "corrections." For you have corrected no one by stealing their property, brutalizing the shackled, or humiliating the handcuffed. The government that does this simply makes people more cynical, colder, and more calculating.

November 1989

B-block days and nightmares

> For whence did Dante take the materials of his hell but
> from our actual world? And yet he made a very proper
> hell of it.
>
> —*Arthur Schopenhauer, "Homo Homini Lupus"**

A shove, a slur, a flurry of punches, and an inmate is cuffed and hustled to the restricted housing unit (RHU), where a beating commences. Wrapped in the sweet, false escape of dreams, I hear the unmistakable sounds of meat being beaten by blackjack, of bootfalls, yells, curses; and it merges into the mind's moviemaking machine, evoking distant memories of some of

---

* From *The World as Will and Representation* by Arthur Schopenhauer, translated by E. F. Payne; Dover Press, 1966.

the Philadelphia Police Department's greatest hits—on me.

"Get off that man, you fat, greasy, racist, red-neck pig bitch muthafucka!"

My tired eyes snap open; the cracks, thuds, "oofs!" come in all too clear. Damn. No dream.

Anger simmers at this abrupt intrusion into one of life's last pleasures on B block—"home" of the state's largest death row—the all-too-brief respite of dreams.

Another dawn, another beating, another shackled inmate pummeled into the concrete by a squadron of guards.

This was late October 1989, the beginning of furious days and nights when prisoners through-out the state erupted in rage. The scene had been replayed a thousand gruesome times, leading to the modest demand that Huntingdon's adminis-trators put an end to beatings of handcuffed pris-oners in B block. The conflict it prompted was ultimately crushed by club and boot, by fire hose and taser electric stun gun.

As walls fall in the Eastern bloc, and as dem-onstrators rejoice over an end to state police brutality, walls climb ever higher in the West. Prisons in America jeer at the rhetoric of liberty espoused by those who now applaud Eastern Europe's glasnost. The U.S. Supreme Court has welded prison doors shut. It has cut off the rights of free press, religion, or civil rights. (See *Shabazz v. O'Lone**** and *Thornburgh v. Abbott*† for examples.) Indeed, in the late 1980s the term "prisoners' rights" became oxymoronic.

The riots that rocked Pennsylvania prisons were flickering reminders of this reality: they were not riots of aggression but of desperation, of men pushed beyond fear, beyond reason, by the clang not only of prison gates but of the slamming of doors to the courthouse, their only legal recourse.

At Huntingdon's A block, fistfights between guard and prisoner evolved into a full-scale riot.

"Walk, you fuckin' nigger! I'm not gonna carry your black ass!"

"You black nigger motherfucker!" Grunts, thuds, groans, and curses assailed the ear as a bloody promenade of cuffed prisoners, many of them the A-block rebels, were dragged, flogged, and flayed down the dirty gray corridors of B

---

* *Estate of Shabazz v. O'Lone* 482 U.S. 342, 107 S.Ct. 2400 (1987).
† *Thornburgh v. Abbott* 490 U.S. 401, 109 S.Ct. 1874 (1989).

block's death row en route to outdoor cages, man-sized dog pens of chain-link fence.

"Officer," a visiting guard barked to a Huntingdon regular, "stop dragging that man!"

"Captain," the local guard answered, her voice pitched higher by rage, "this fuckin' nigger don't wanna walk!"

The prisoners were herded into cages—most bloody, some in underwear, all wet, all exposed to the night air for hours.

Days later, Camp Hill in central Pennsylvania erupted, with prisoners taking hostages, assaulting some, and putting much of the forty-eight-year-old facility to the torch. For two nights the state's most overcrowded prison stole the public's attention. It took a battery of guards and state troopers to wrest back some semblance of control.

"Say 'I'm a nigger!' Say it!" the baton-wielders taunted black prisoners, beating those who refused according to MOVE political prisoner and eyewitness Chuck Africa, who, although not a participant in the rebellion, was nonetheless beaten by guards.

Days after the fires of Camp Hill cooled, while convicts stood shackled together in the soot-covered yard, Philadelphia's Holmesburg burst into its worst riot in almost twenty years. At its peak, prisoners yelled, "Camp Hill! Camp Hill!"

Now, as costs for "Camp Hell" 's reconstruction soar (latest estimate: $21 million), and bills are introduced to cover county costs for riot prosecutions (to the tune of $1.25 million), one must question the predictably conventional wisdom attributing the days and nights of rage to simple overcrowding. To be sure, the system's "jam and cram" policy was a factor, but only one among many.

In 1987 the Governor's Interdepartmental Task Force on Corrections, composed of eight cabinet-level secretaries, issued a comprehensive report calling for changes in the state's prisons: reform of the misconduct system, institution of earnest (known as "good") time, liberalization of visiting procedures, release of death row prisoners from the RHU, and introduction of substantial education programs. The report, despite its pedigree, died a pauper's death, its biggest promises unfulfilled.

The naming of David Owens, Jr., as prison commissioner in 1987, the first black in the top post, may have heightened expectations, especially among blacks, who make up 56 percent of the prison population, but it also deepened frustrations. Prisoners saw no change in rule by predominantly rural whites over predominantly urban Afros and Latinos. Was it mere coincidence that rebellion burned hottest at Camp Hill, within sight of the commissioner's office?

Owens's tenure proved as short-lived as it was historic. Politicians protested when he proposed nominal compensation for prisoners who lost their property in the state's shakedown after the riots. Mindful of looming gubernatorial elections and of politicians angling to make Owens and the prisons an issue, Pennsylvania's first-term, socially conservative governor, Robert Casey, accepted Owens's resignation. With the state's captive population breaking twenty-one thousand, prisons overcrowded by 50 percent, and more than seven hundred convicts in the federal system, it's not surprising that there are now no takers for Owens's politically sensitive job.

Perhaps there is a certain symmetry in the circumstance of a prison system in crisis in the very state where the world's first true penitentiary arose, under Quaker influence. Two hundred years after initiation of this grim experiment, it is clear that it has failed.*

One state representative (since criticized by her colleagues for making "irresponsible" statements) boldly told United Press International the simple hidden truth. Unless serious change is forthcoming, she predicted, "we are going to continue to have riots."

Repression is not change; it's the same old stuff.

The Nation *April 1990*

---

* Quaker prison experiment, Walnut St. Penitentiary 1790, Philadelphia, Pennsylvania.

part two

Crime and punishment

Human waste camps

A dark, repressive trend in the business field known as "corrections" is sweeping the United States, and it bodes ill both for the captives and for the communities from which they were captured.

America is revealing a visage stark with harshness. Nowhere is that face more contorted than in the dark netherworld of prison, where humans are transformed into nonpersons, numbered beings cribbed into boxes of unlife, where the very soul is under destructive onslaught.

We are in the midst of the Marionization* of U.S. prisons, where the barest illusion of human rehabilitation is stripped from the mission, to be

---

* "Marionization" coined in Human Rights Watch Report. Prison conditions in the U.S. 1991. In 1983 Marion Federal Penitentiary became a permanent lockdown control unit. The forebear and model of Super Max prisons in thirty-eight states. Three of the newest control unit prisons are in Pelican Bay, California; Florence, Colorado; and Greene County, Pennsylvania.

replaced by dehumanization by design. As prison populations swell to bursting, states scramble for funds to construct new control units, known by a variety of names: RHU, SMU, SHU, Supermax. Their public relations spokesmen defend such units as rural, isolated reserves for the "worst of the worst."

That justification was the basis for the infamous lockdown of the Marion federal penitentiary, where the government promptly dumped a number of political prisoners, including, for a time at least, former Black Panther Sundiata Acoli, former American Indian Movement activist Leonard Peltier, former resistance conspiracy defendant Dr. Alan Berkman, and North American anti-imperialist Tim Blunk, among others. In 1987, Amnesty International reported that Marion violates almost every one of the United Nations' Standard Minimum Rules for the Treatment of Prisoners. Several TV networks recently reported on the Pelican Bay, California, Supermax, a state torture chamber called Skeleton Bay by prisoners. In Pennsylvania, a so-called special management unit (SMU) was built in a rural, financially strapped area, where the state specializes in shriveling the soul. It seems to specialize also in punishing jailhouse lawyers, and serves as punishment for those who had the nerve to win civil and criminal suits. Consider one case: Dennis "Solo" McKeithan explains his history before being sent to the SMU. "From June 1985 to November 1, 1989, I never went to the hole while in prison and never had a misconduct more serious than two sticks of reefer. I went three years without any kind of misconduct while engaging in studies, [being] a literacy tutor and all." In March 1992, all that changed after Solo was charged with hitting a nurse at Huntingdon prison. Shortly thereafter, the writer saw him locked in a cage on B block, his left eye swollen to the size of a golf ball.

In an astonishing, unexpected event, Solo was tried and *acquitted* (Yes!) on November 13, 1992, by an all-white, rural Huntingdon County jury, who disbelieved the (white) nurse's tale.

On November 17, 1992, despite the acquittal, Solo was shipped to the SMU and locked down.

Now having lost eighteen pounds since his arrival, he battles for his freedom, and dignity, against a system designed to deny both.

September 1993

Black march to death

Every day in America the trek continues, a black march to death row.

In Pennsylvania, where African-Americans constitute 9 percent of the population, over 60 percent of its death row inhabitants are black. Across the nation, although the numbers are less stark, the trend is unmistakable. In October 1991 the Bureau of Justice Statistics released its national update, which revealed that 40 percent of America's death row population is black. This, out of a population that is a mere 11 percent of the national populace. The five states with the largest death rows have larger percentages on death row than in their statewide black populations.

Statistics are often flexible in interpretation and, like scripture, can be cited for any purpose. Does this mean that African-Americans are somehow innocents, subjected to a setup by state officials? Not especially. What it does suggest is that state actors, at all stages of the criminal justice system, including slating at the police station, arraignment at the judicial office, pre-trial, trial, and sentencing stage before a court, treat African-American defendants with a special vengeance not experienced by white defendants.

This is the dictionary definition of "discrimination."

In the 1987 case *McCleskey v. Kemp*, the famed Baldus study revealed facts that unequivocally proved the following*: (1) defendants charged with killing white victims in Georgia are 4.3 times as likely to be sentenced to death as defendants charged with killing blacks; (2) six of every eleven defendants convicted of killing a white person would not have received the death sentence if their victim had been black; and (3) cases involving black defendants and white victims are more likely to result in a death sentence than cases featuring any other racial combination of defendant and victim.

Although the U.S. Supreme Court, by a 5 to 4

---

* *McCleskey v. Kemp* 481 U.S. 279 (1987); quoted verbatim.

vote, rejected McCleskey's claims, it could hardly reject the facts underlying them.

Retired Justice Powell said in essence that "differences don't amount to discrimination."

The bedrock reason that McCleskey was denied relief was the fear, again expressed by Powell, that "McCleskey's claim, taken to its logical conclusion, throws into serious question the principles that underlie our entire criminal justice system." How true. *McCleskey* can't be correct, or else the whole system is incorrect.

Now that couldn't be the case, could it?

December 1991

Slavery daze II

A specter haunts America's black communities. Vampirish, it sucks the souls out of black lives, leaving skeletal husks behind, mobile, animated, but emotionally and spiritually dead. This is not the result of a dark Count Drac attack, nor a spell woven by a sinister shaman; it is the direct result of global greed, governmental deception, and the eternal longing of the poor to escape, however briefly, from the crippling shackles of utter poverty.

Their quest for relief is spelled C-R-A-C-K. Crack. Rock. Call it what you will, it is, in truth, another word for "death" in African-American communities.

Harvested in Latin America's Peruvian highlands, treated in jungle labs, "cured" in a chemical bath of ether and kerosene, carried into the U.S.A. by government-hired pilots as a way to pay the fledgling contras' bills, cocaine comes to Chocolate City, U.S.A., and, transformed into crystalline crack, wreaks havoc on poor black life. Forgotten by the federal government, stigmatized by the state government, shunted aside, ignored, or exploited by city governments, the poor are perceived as problems, or ostracized as alien others, beyond the social pale, anything but *people* who are not provided the basic tools of survival. It is these poor folks, locked in American Bantustans, who have fallen the hardest for crack.

Just as the "Just Say No" generation got down from the political stage, tons of a new potent poison were being peddled in poor sections of town, brought to these shores courtesy of the Iran-contra funds diversion scheme, as masterminded by that great American hero Honest Ollie North (known as Operation Black Eagle—CIA). Why would the government (the same government that says "Just Say No") dare bring cocaine into the States, if not to sell it, to turn it into lucre, into cold cash? If their intent was to destroy it, this could have easily been done outside the U.S.A. It was not destroyed. I suspect an ulterior motive.

Recent history, back in the radical 1960s, saw a flood of pills, pot, and high-grade heroin into black neighborhoods. Radicals suspected then that the malevolent hand of Big Brother opened the floodgates of drugs to drown out the black revolutionary fires of urban resistance.

With a hostile U.S. Supreme Court, growing unemployment, a federal government that "kindly" and "gently" turned its back on the homeless, police forces marauding like Green Berets over inner cities, African-American resistance seems a likely response.

Open the floodgates, again—this time with a potent, mind-sucking, soul-ripping poison that takes utter priority over all else. The natural instinct of motherhood melts into mud next to the pangs of the crack attack.

Babies are being sold, and mothers sell themselves, in homage to the plastic vial.

Homes disintegrate into New Age caves under the spell of the 'caine. Families fall apart, as fathers are herded into newly built prisons and mothers haunt ho-strolls, all in an infernal lust for that sweet, deadly poison.

There is a precedent for such a diabolical scheme in U.S. history. How many Native

"American" communities and tribes were devastated by the European introduction of "fire water" (alcohol, rum, etc.) into the tribal diet, and indeed wiped out?

This is a dire hour for Africans in the United States.

Will we survive this plague?

July 1989

Skeleton bay

Distrust anyone in whom the desire to punish is powerful.

—*Friedrich Nietzsche*

As of 1993, according to U.S. Bureau of Justice statistics, there were 119,951 people including parolees imprisoned in California.* At last count, California had over twenty-eight prisons and spends over $1 *b*illion annually ($1,000,000,000!) on prisons. One billion! And then there's Pelican Bay prison, a hellish home for thirty-seven hundred prisoners, located in an isolated rural area called Crescent City, California. If Pelican Bay prison is a hell,† then its special housing unit

---

* A recent *New York Times* poll shows that more than one million people are now in U.S. state and federal prisons.

† In January 1995 the U.S. District Court held the state could continue operating Pelican Bay, and while the U.S. District Judge Thelton Henderson was critical of the unit, he declined to declare it unconstitutional, despite evidence that guards inflicted unjustified beatings upon and hog-tying of prisoners.

(SHU), commonly called SHOE, is the lower depths, where nearly thirteen hundred men are consigned to a state program of torture and governmental terrorism, so much so that major news agencies, such as CBS's *60 Minutes*, have reported on the unit.

Prisoners there haven't taken the abusive treatment lying down, as evidenced by a civil suit filed in federal court, charging the state with "lawless" activity. "The law stops at the gates of Pelican Bay," attorney Susan Creighton told the court in her opening argument late September in San Francisco. At the SHU, men are beaten, burned, and isolated by state officers. Prisoners spend twenty-two and a half hours a day in windowless eight-by-ten cells, with no human contact or educational opportunities.

One defense psychologist, Dr. Craig Haney, found "chronic depression, hallucinations and thought disorders" at levels existing at no other prison in the United States. The symptoms were comparable only to findings from a psychiatric prison in the former East Germany, known for torture and solitary confinement, Haney testified. Indeed, the conditions are so horrendous that a former warden of the infamous hellhole Marion, Illinois, openly criticized Pelican, tracing a record of numerous injuries and deaths to guards' routine use of excessive force.

Charles E. Fenton, ex-warden of Marion Federal Penitentiary testified in the suit, "There seems to be an attitude ... that it's proper for staff to shoot at inmates" (*San Francisco Chronicle*, September 29, 1993).

"They either absolutely don't know what they're doing or they're deliberately inflicting pain," said Fenton.

Marion Federal Penitentiary, known as Son of Alcatraz, was itself condemned as violative of fundamental human rights by Amnesty International. Pelican Bay (called Skeleton Bay by prisoners) is Son of Marion, taken to such an inhumane degree that even Marion's old warden gasps in shock at the ugliness that is his spawn. Five years from now, will we be moaning about the Son of Pelican?

If we don't rumble now, against *all* fascistic control units, such as Pelican, Pennsylvania's SMU, Shawnee Unit at Marianna, Florida, and

Colorado State Penitentiary, you may not be able to rumble later.

The solution is not in the courts but in an awake, aware people.

October 1993

No law, no rights

A federal civil rights trial in Philadelphia charging seven former Graterford prison guards with violating the civil rights of a number of prisoners by severely beating them, while they were shackled and cuffed hand and foot, in November 1989, revealed in glaring fashion how, in prisons, there is no law—there are no rights.

Despite the guilty pleas and damning testimony of five ex-guards, that they and their colleagues maliciously beat, kicked, stomped, blackjacked, and tasered (that is, used a handheld electric shocking device) prisoners who committed no institutional offenses, a civil jury acquitted the seven of virtually all charges in February 1993.

One juror was quoted as saying that although it was proven that prisoners were badly beaten, no conspiracy was proven by U.S. prosecutors.

One prisoner who suffered from AIDS, and thus had fewer internal resources with which to rebound from the horrific physical and psychological trauma he suffered in the beating, has since died.

The monthlong trial revealed that guards thought nineteen prisoners who were transferred from Camp Hill prison shortly after rioters and rebels nearly leveled the central Pennsylvania facility to a pile of smouldering ashes were part of the rioting crews that ripped it apart. In fact, the nineteen were nonrioters, who were only too glad to be leaving what came to be called Camp Hell, and to be coming to the state's largest, and blackest, prison: Graterford.

Instead, they were leaving the fire only to get simmered in the frying pan, so to speak.

At Graterford, whose massive haunting walls seemed to offer some relief from the raging literal and psychic infernos of Camp Hill, the nineteen men met uniformed hatred and naked brutality, as they were beaten, kicked, and terrorized by government officials sworn to protect the illusive "peace" in prisons—guards who, acting on nothing but assumptions, assaulted over a dozen men on the notion that they were troublemakers. Some, those few who could navigate the treacherous straits and shoals of civil litigation, sued state officials for damages. Others bound up their wounds and blended into the wall while waiting for terms to expire, so they could be "free" again. Several testified in the federal prosecution.

One died.

But all found out how fragile the very system that stole their very freedom was when the state committed crimes against them. All found out that words like "justice," "law," "civil rights," and, yes, "crime" have different and elastic meanings depending on whose rights were violated, who committed what crimes against whom, and whether one works for the system or against it.

For those people, almost a million at last count, who wear the label "prisoner" around their necks, there is no law, there is no justice, there are no rights.

February 1993

Two bites of the
apple in Dixie

Last term, the U.S. Supreme Court delivered a
full, foul package of repressive rulings, but perhaps none was more obscene than *Penry v.
Lynaugh*, where the Court stamped its seal of approval on the execution of the mentally retarded.
In *Penry*, the Rehnquist right wing, represented
by Justice O'Connor, justified its decision by pro-
claiming that "no national consensus exists" op-
posing capital punishment for the retarded. *Penry*
represents the clearest instance of "justice" by
"public opinion poll," also known as "national
consensus," now holding sway in America's court
of last resort.* As it happened, however, the
Court's majority was dead wrong.

---

* *Penry v. Lynaugh*, 492 U.S. S.Ct., 302 106 L.Ed.2d 256 (1989).

In a recently published *National Law Journal/LEXIS* crime poll, conducted by Penn and Schoen Associates of New York, the figures reveal an overwhelming majority of Americans, 69 percent, *oppose* the death penalty for retarded persons (*NLJ*, August 7, 1989). The poll suggests, on this issue at least, that the Court's rightist majority is simply out of step with America's majority. Such statistics, however, are hollow where life and death are concerned.

For Horace Dunkins, Jr., who was strapped into Alabama's electric chair on July 14, 1989, shortly past midnight, it had no meaning at all. Horace Dunkins was retarded. His meager IQ matched the percentage of Americans who opposed his legalized murder—69. But if the dictionary definition of "retarded" (slow or limited intellect) has any relevance here, surely the Alabama Department of Corrections should qualify. Dunkins was electrocuted—twice. At 12:08 A.M., the executioner flipped the switch, sending manmade lightning surging through Dunkins. The doctors found the man alive, unconscious. Perhaps it is fitting that Alabama's "Corrections" Department could not correctly execute an execution, without torturing its charge. Alabama

107

legally killed Dunkins* with the blessing of the U.S. Supreme Court's 5 to 4 majority.

In a series of articles written by Dunkins's lawyer, Stephen D. Ellis, in Philadelphia's *Legal Intelligencer*,† the fundamental unfairness of Dunkins's fate, and the nightmarish details of his double electrocution, are recounted, in a case Ellis called a "miscarriage of justice." For most Americans, one electrocution is the stuff of mystery, as most have never witnessed it. For most it is a forbidden zone, an act committed in the dark far from the madding crowd, an act accomplished in a state of stealth.

Several decades ago, a celebrated justice of the Pennsylvania Supreme Court did witness an execution by electrocution, and wrote:

He started, painfully and uncertainly, to lower himself into the chair, but now the guards were swift. They lifted him deep into the seat and ad-

---

* Peter Applebome, *Two Electric Jolts in Alabama Execution, New York Times*, July 15, 1989, p. 6. Philadelphia's *Legal Intelligencer*, Stephen D. Ellis articles about executions of mentally ill and his client Horace Dunkins, Jr., executed by the state of Alabama, July 14, 1989.

† S. D. Ellis, *The Execution of Horace Dunkin's Jr.* (Parts 1 and 2); *The Legal Intelligencer*, (8/23/89-8/24/89), p. 9.

justed the electrodes at calves and wrists. Then they fastened a thick belt across his chest and lowered over his head the heavy wired leather mask. It hid all but the tip of his nose and his lips. He was making efforts to quiet them by biting his tongue, the best that he could do, against his racing mind and heart, to keep control and to sit erect. . . .*

Then Justice Bok goes to the meat of his blow-by-blow recap:

The guards stepped back. The Warden, who had stood by with arms raised, lowered his hand. It had taken a minute and thirty-seven seconds.

There was a low whine and a short loud snap, as of huge teeth closing. Roger's head flew back and his body leaped forward against the confining straps. Almost at once smoke arose from his head and left wrist and was sucked up into the ventilator overhead. The body churned against the bonds, and the lips ceased trembling and turned red, then

---

* Though taken from Bok's *Star Wormwood*, text was found by the author at Op. A.G. No. 1 (1971), *Opinions of the Attorney General*; Commonwealth of Pennsylvania, p. 5 citing opinion of former Attorney General Fred Speaker; the Attorney General in 1971 was J. Shane Creamer.

slowly changed to blue. Moisture appeared on the skin and a sizzling noise was audible. The smell of burning flesh grew heavy in the air.

Roger was being broiled.

The current went off with a distinct clap after about two minutes and Roger slumped back into his seat, his head hanging. No one moved. Then came the second jolt and again the body surged against the restraining straps and smoke rose from it. The visible flesh was turkey red.

Again the current slammed off and this time the doctor stepped forward to listen, but he moved back again and shook his head. Apparently Roger still clung faintly to life.

The third charge struck him, and again the smoking and sizzling and broiling. His flesh was swelling around the straps. The doctor listened carefully and raised his head. "I pronounce this man dead," he said, folding up his stethoscope. It was seven minutes after Roger had been seated in the chair.

—*Star Wormwood*, 114–115

Thirty years after Justice Bok's eerie description of the Keystone State's triple electrocution, America makes "progress," at a snail's pace, with the torturous double electrocution of Horace Dunkins, a retarded black man in Alabama. While the state of Georgia barred the execution of mentally retarded folks, its sister state, "the heart of Dixie," did not have such a law, and in its fourth execution since reinstatement of the death penalty in 1976, it has presented a spectacle of heartlessness and utter incompetence. Even supporters of capital punishment, faced with the torturous double frying of Horace Dunkins, must mutter to themselves, "Do it right, dammit—or don't do it at all!"

August 1989

Blackmun bows out
of the death game

Harry A. Blackmun, the U.S. Supreme Court's senior justice, has finally held, as a matter of constitutional law, that the death penalty, as currently administered, is unconstitutional.

Blackmun, in a dissenting opinion in the case *Callins v. Collins** announced his position in a lengthy dissent that was severely critical of the majority of the Court for "having virtually conceded that both fairness and rationality cannot be achieved" in their death penalty cases, adding, "The Court has chosen to deregulate the entire enterprise, replacing, it would seem, substantive constitutional requirements with mere aesthetics. . . ."

In what appeared to be judicial bitterness,

---

* *Callins v. Collins* 114 S.Ct. 1127 (1994); quotes verbatim.

Blackmun further announced, "From this day forward, I no longer shall tinker with the machinery of death."

The Blackmun dissent, which recounts Supreme Court precedent from its death docket, is a grim telling of judicial restrictions; cases stemming from the 1976 case *Gregg v. Georgia*,* which reinstated the death penalty, to more recent ones, such as *Herrera v. Collins*,† where the Court denied a hearing to a man trying to prove innocence.

But if Blackmun's denunciation of his benchmates seemed bitter, the response of some on death row seemed equally acerbic.

"Why now?" asked one.

"What's it mean?" asked another.

Blackmun's trek, from *Gregg v. Georgia*, where the death penalty was reinstated, to *Callins v. Collins*, where he condemned capital punishment to unconstitutionality, in a singular dissent, comes almost a quarter century too late for many in the shadow of the death house. His principled refusal to further "tinker with the machinery of death" comes after the machine has been fine-

---

* *Gregg v. Georgia* 96 S.Ct. 128 U.S. 153, 49 L.Ed.2d 859 (1976).
† *Herrera v. Collins*, 113 S.Ct. 853 (1993).

tuned and stripped to its malevolent best, after all of its bugs have been purged and a pit crew installed to keep it running well into the next century.

Blackmun's critical fifth vote in the *Gregg* case made the death penalty possible and formed the foundation for the plethora of cases now condemned in *Callins*, like *McCleskey*, *Herrera*, *Sawyer*,* and others, for without *Gregg*, the others would not be. Further, his dissent, although remarkable in its passioned discourse, is of negligible legal force and will save not one life, not even defendant Callins. Blackmun, in his death penalty jurisprudence at least, assumes the late Justice Marshall's mantle of the lone dissenter, a Jeremiah preaching in a dry, searing judicial wilderness, where few will hear and none will follow.

Had he joined Marshall while he lived, and Brennan while he adjudicated, a life bloc might have emerged, with enough light and enough strength to fashion a majority by attracting two stragglers, but this never occurred and, he suggests in his dissent in *Callins*, may never occur. He wrote:

---

* *Sawyer v. Whitley* 112 S.Ct. 2514 (1994).

Perhaps one day this Court will develop procedural rules or verbal formulas that actually will provide consistency, fairness, and reliability in a capital-sentencing scheme. I am not optimistic that such a day will come. I am more optimistic though, that this Court eventually will conclude that the effort to eliminate arbitrariness while preserving fairness in the infliction of [death] is so plainly doomed to failure that it—and the death penalty—must be abandoned altogether. I may not live to see that day, but I have faith that eventually it will arrive.

To which some on death row respond, "No time soon."

March 1994

Jury of peers?

In all criminal prosecutions, the accused shall enjoy the right to a speedy and public trial, *by an impartial jury* of the state and district wherein the crime shall have been committed. . . .

—*Sixth Amendment, U.S. Constitution*

Much of the propaganda beamed around the world proclaims the glories of U.S. democracy, such as "free" elections, representative government, and trial by jury. The following is assuredly not broadcast.

William Henry Hance* was convicted of killing a Georgia prostitute back in 1978 and sentenced to death. His trial, and even his subsequent retrial, took place before predominantly white juries. One of those jurors, the only black juror, filed a sworn affidavit that she never agreed to the death sentence, a claim seconded

---

* *Hance v. Zant* 114 S.Ct. 1392 (1994).

116

by another, white juror. The second juror paints a picture of a trial that was more a lynching than a legal proceeding.

This juror, Pamela Lemay, swore in a notarized affidavit that she heard another white juror, a woman, state, "The nigger admitted he did it, he should fry." At several instances, at the hotel, and during deliberations out of the black juror's presence, Ms. Lemay swore she heard other white jurors refer to Hance as "a typical nigger" and "just one more sorry nigger that no one would miss." During deliberations as to whether Hance should be executed or sentenced to life, a juror remarked that execution would be best because that way, "there'd be one less nigger to breed."

This, in America, is the true meaning of a "jury of peers."

Did any of this bother either the Georgia superior court, the Georgia Supreme Court, the U.S. Supreme Court, or the Georgia Board of Pardons and Paroles?

Absolutely not.

On April 31, 1994, at 10 P.M., William Henry Hance, a man both retarded and mentally ill, was executed, that is, "legally lynched," by the government of Georgia—by electrocution.

117

Georgia's state motto is "Wisdom, Justice, and Moderation." In the case of William Henry Hance, these three elements seemed sorely lacking.

In an emergency appeal to the U.S. Supreme Court hours before Hance's electrocution, Justice Blackmun, in a dissenting opinion in Hance's case, wrote that even if he hadn't "reached the conclusion that the death penalty cannot be imposed fairly within the constraints of our constitution . . . I could not support its imposition in this case." Quoth Blackmun: "There is substantial evidence that William Henry Hance is mentally retarded as well as mentally ill. There is reason to believe that his trial and sentencing proceedings were infected with racial prejudice. One of his sentencers has come forward to say that she did not vote for the death penalty because of his mental impairments."

A majority of the Supreme Court rejected this reasoning. And in the last analysis, the courts and agencies of both Georgia and the United States agreed with the anonymous juror at his trial who believed that Hance would be better off dead, that his death would mean "one less nigger to breed."

April 1994

Expert witness from hell

In 1987, a twenty-eight-year-old West Virginia cemetery worker, Glen Dale Woodall, was convicted of the vicious, brutal kidnapping and rape of two women. His life almost ended when a judge sentenced him to two life terms, with an additional 325-year sentence for the crimes.

The evidence was convincing: the state's medical examiner testified that Woodall's semen was found in both victims. Medical examiners, like all expert witnesses, are accorded high respect in American courts, for they are thought to be totally impartial, and only an ally of science. In Woodall's case, the testimony of medical examiner Fred Zain was the key that locked him away in a dim prison cell for the rest of his natural life. There was only one problem: Zain, forensic expert for the West Virginia State Police for over a decade, was wrong.

After Woodall spent almost five years in prison, his lawyer, Lonnie Simmons, took a long shot by having remnants of the semen found in the victims tested by the new DNA method. The tests proved conclusively that Woodall's semen did not match the samples. Woodall, sentenced to two life terms, plus 325 years, was innocent.

The West Virginia Supreme Court ordered an examination of the forensic expert's testing in other cases and came up with the startling conclusion that Zain's work was systematically deficient, entering the following ruling: "Any testimony or documentary evidence offered by Zain, at any time, in any criminal prosecution, should be deemed invalid, unreliable and inadmissible."

For thirteen years, Zain testified in hundreds of rape and murder trials in West Virginia, and later performed similarly in San Antonio, Texas, affecting, according to one attorney's estimate, more than forty-five hundred criminal cases in two states.

In 1990, a handyman, Jack Davis, was sentenced to life in prison for the 1989 murder and mutilation of a central Texas woman. Zain testified at Davis's trial that blood found under the

120

victim's body placed the defendant at the scene. Davis's lawyer, Stanley Schneider, proved that, in fact, no test was done. Zain, according to forensic specialists in both states, wrote reports on tests that were never done, reported positive matches where negatives would have cleared suspects, and listed as "conclusive" test results that were inconclusive. His efforts to please cops and prosecutors sent possibly thousands of innocent men to serve centuries in prisons across two states, some on death row.

As of this writing, the ex–medical examiner hasn't been charged with a single offense in either state. His lawyer, Larry Souza, laments that Zain's life has been "ruined. He can't find a job in his profession. He's been reduced to working as a common laborer. He has nowhere to go."

I'm sure several thousand prisoners in West Virginia and Texas have some ideas about where to send him.

May 1994

The demand for death

Death row prisoner Michael Alan Durocher of Florida sent a letter to the governor, literally begging to be executed. When Governor Lawton Chiles signed his death warrant, Durocher sent him a thank-you note. On August 25, 1993, at 7:15 A.M., Durocher, thirty-three, got his wish.

California's death row convict David Mason fired his appellate lawyers, stating his willingness to die in the gas chamber. Mason, thirty-six, was angrily critical of what he called the "industry" of lawyers capitalizing off of capital appeals. Despite his eleventh-hour conversion from his previous determination to die, the Mason case came to symbolize the apparently growing occurrence of death row prisoners who demand death. The case also demonstrates the difference between popular perception and reality.

Of the approximately twenty-seven hundred men and women on U.S. death rows, only twenty-six people, less than 1 percent, have volunteered to be executed. The Washington, D.C.–based National Coalition to Abolish the Death Penalty has assembled data detailing the racial breakdown of those opting for execution, and found the following:

Race of Prisoners	Number	Percentage
White	21	80.8
Black	2	7.7
Latino	2	7.7
Not available	1	3.8

Whites constitute less than 51 percent of all death row prisoners in the United States but make up over 80 percent of all volunteers for execution. Why?

Nationally, African-Americans mark roughly 40 percent of the U.S. death row population and 46 percent of state prisoners.

Increasingly, since the rebellious 1960s, prison populations have become blacker and blacker, a reality that can be perceived only as threatening and fearful to the average white prisoner. For far too many blacks, prisons have become a warped

123

rite of passage, a malevolent mark of manhood, and a dark expectation.

For whites, however, even working-class whites, prison is a mark of social expulsion in extremis, and an affirmation of one's outcast status. Blacks have a longer history of rejection from this society than the relatively recent era of grudging acceptance. Many have been socialized into oppression, with prison just one more grim experience, in a bitter existence.

What all share equally, however, is the relentless regime of lockdown, loneliness, isolation, and hopelessness while one awaits death, exacting a terrible psychic, spiritual, psychological, and familial toll. A flight to death, then, is often a flight from the soul-killing conditions of death row.

September 1993

Already out of the game

The newest political fever sweeping the nation, the "three strikes, you're out" rage, will, barring any last-minute changes, become law in the United States, thereby opening the door to a state-by-state march to an unprecedented prison building boom. What most politicians know, however, is what most people do not—that "three strikes, you're out" will do next to nothing to eradicate crime, and will not create the illusive dream of public safety.

They also know that it will be years before the bills come due, but when they do, they'll be real doozies; by then, they reason, they'll be out of office, and it'll be another politician's problem. That's because the actual impact of "three strikes" will not be felt for at least ten to twenty years from now, simply because that's the range someone arrested today would face already (under the current laws), and the additional time, not to mention additional costs, will kick in then.

It seems a tad superfluous to state that already some thirty-four states have habitual offender (so-called career criminal) laws, which call for additional penalties on the second, not the third, felony, in addition to the actual crime. As with every law, taxpayers will have to "pay the cost to be the boss." Pennsylvanians are paying over $600 million this fiscal year for their prisons; Californians, over $2.7 billion this year, with costs for next year expected to top costs for higher education.

As prisons become increasingly geriatric, with populations hitting their fifties and sixties, those already atmospheric costs will balloon exponentially for expected health costs, so that although many Americans, an estimated thirty-seven million, don't have guaranteed health care, prisoners will, although of doubtful quality.

Frankly, it's always amazing to see politicians sell their "We-gotta-get-tough-on-crime" schtick to a country that is already the world's leading incarcerator, and perhaps more amazing to see the country buy it. One state has already trod that tough ground, back in the 1970s; California "led" the nation in 1977 with their tough "determinate sentencing" law, and their prison population exploded over 500 percent, from 22,486 in 1973 to 119,000 in 1993, now boasting the largest prison system in the Western world—50 percent larger than the entire federal prison system. Do Californians—rushing to pass the "three strikes, you're out" ballot initiative— feel safer?

A more cynical soul, viewing this prison-boom bill through the lens of economic interest, might suppose that elements of the correctional industry, builders, guards' unions, and the like are fueling the boom, at least in part.

Another element is the economy itself, where America enters the postindustrial age, when Japan produces the world's computer chips; Germany produces high performance autos; and America produces . . . prisons. Prisons are where America's jobs programs, housing programs, and social control programs merge into a dark whole; and where those already outside of the game can be exploited and utilized to keep the game going.

March 1994

A bill that is a crime

The so-called crime bill, that profane political expletive, is now the law. Packing some sixty-odd death penalties, a "three strikes, you're out" provision, and billions of bucks for cops and prisons, the crime bill, as proposed by President Clinton, was an act so Draconian that neither presidents Bush nor Reagan could have successfully passed such a measure. The bill is, in essence, a $30+ billion public employment program for predominantly white workers, a social program if ever there was one that reflects the changing face of America's sociopolitical and economic reality.

So nakedly political was the fight for the bill's passage, that it boiled down to a misleading equation of "pork" vs. "toughness." Republicans attacked the bill as "pork"; Democrats touted it as "tough on crime"; while both sides were merely seeking partisan advantage for the fall campaigns.

It is the purest pork to call for building prisons in a nation that leads the entire world in imprisonment of its citizens. The outbreaks of criminal cops uncovered by the New York Mollen Commission reveals that the equation "more cops = less crime" is both simplistic and erroneous. This is porkchopish in the extreme.

For prisoners, the crime bill outlaws knowledge, because it prohibits government funds for college courses, as the following provision notes;

Sec. 20411. *Awards of Pell Grants to Prisoners Prohibited.*

"(a) *In General.*—Section 401(b)(8) of the Higher Education Act of 1965 (20 U.S.C. 1070.a.(b)(8)) is amended to read as follows:

"(8) No basic grant shall be awarded under the subpart to any individual who is incarcerated in any federal or state penal institution.

How any member of Congress can, in good faith, reason that human ignorance fights crime or protects society is beyond comprehension. Indeed, it can be said that ignorance is the mother of all crime.

But the ideologically driven drivel that is the

crime bill, this dark political ticket for reelection, will bite the asses of Americans for generations to come. It will drive public bankruptcy; it will fuel greater violence; it will create prisoners who are dumber, more alienated, but more desperate in life's scuffle for survival.

Consider this: The drugged-out zombie about to rob you calculates the worth of stealing your property versus four to eight years in prison, if caught. Factor in your property versus life without parole, and your life, not your property, is devalued.

That swift and fatal calculation is being tallied hourly in cities from coast to coast, and the so-called crime bill just made it more costly—for you.

September 1994

part three

Musings, memories, and prophecies

Musings on Malcolm

Thanks to the efforts of premier filmmaker Spike Lee, the name Malcolm X is once again on millions of lips. Based largely on the *Autobiography of Malcolm X*, penned by the late Alex Haley, the film tells the epic tale of a man who was indeed larger than life.

This is not, and cannot be, a film review, for I have never seen the film, for reasons that should be obvious. Rather, it is a musing on the life that gave both Haley and Spike grist for their mills.

Few black men lived a life as full of glory and tragedy as did he; Martin Luther King, Jr., did; and to a lesser extent so did Marcus Garvey, as well as the late Black Panther cofounder Dr. Huey P. Newton. As were King and Newton, Malcolm X was assassinated, but perhaps the similarity ends there. For as America lionized, lauded, and elevated King (more for his non-

violent philosophy than for his person), it ignored and ignominized Malcolm (as it did Dr.
Newton, a Malcolmite, as were most Panthers),
whose obituaries dwelt on the dark side, ignoring the brilliance of his life, a force that still
smoulders in black hearts thirty years after his
assassination in New York City.

The system used the main nonviolent themes
of Martin Luther King's life to present a strategy
designed to protect its own interests—imagine
the most violent nation on earth, the heir of
Indian and African genocide, the *only* nation ever
to drop an atomic bomb on a civilian population,
the world's biggest arms dealer, the country that
napalmed over ten million people in Vietnam (to
"save" it from communism), the world's biggest
jailer, waving the corpse of King, calling for non-
violence!

The Black Panther Party considered itself the
Sons of Malcolm (at least many male Panthers
did) for the sons he never had (Malcolm and his
wife, Dr. Betty Shabazz, had a passel of stunning
daughters), and inherited one of their central
tenets, black self-defense, from his teachings.

While the eloquent, soaring oratory of Dr.
King touched, moved, and motivated the south-

134

ern black church, middle and upper classes, and white liberal predominantly Jewish intelligentsia, his message did not find root in the black working class and urban north, a fact noted by his brilliant, devoted aide-de-camp the Reverend Ralph Abernathy, who noted in his autobiography that in Chicago King met glacial white hatred, black indifference, and near disaster.

Northern-bred blacks preferred a more defiant, confrontational, and militant message than turn the other cheek, and Malcolm X provided it in clear, uncompromising terms. His message of black self-defense and African-American self-determination struck both Muslim and non-Muslim alike as logical and reasonable, given the decidedly unchristian behavior displayed by America to the black, brown, red, and yellow world.

The media, as Malcolm predicted, would attempt to homogenize, whiten, and distort his message. How many have read of him, in a recent newspaper, described as a "civil rights" leader—a term he loathed! Stories tell of his "softening" toward whites after his sojourn to Mecca, conveniently ignoring that Malcolm continued to revile white *Americans*, still in the

135

grips of a racist *system* that crushes black life—
still! Post-Mecca Malik found among white-
skinned Arabs and European converts to Islam a
oneness that he found lacking in Americans. So
deeply entrenched was racism in American
whites that Malcolm/Malik sensed the intrinsic
difference in how the two peoples saw and described themselves. Arabs, calling themselves
white, referred simply to skin tone; Americans
meant something altogether different: "You
know what he means when he says 'I'm white,'
he means he's *boss*!" Malcolm thundered.

Malcolm, and the man who returned from
Mecca, Hajji Malik Shabazz, both were scourges
of American racism who saw it as an evil against
humanity and the God that formed them. He
stood for—and died for—*human* rights of self-
defense and a people's self-determination, not
for "civil rights," which, as the Supreme Court
has indeed shown, changes from day to day, case
to case, administration to administration.

December 1992

Deadly déjà vu

After fifty-one days of remarkable religious resistance, the U.S. government eliminated over
eighty members of the Branch Davidian sect
near Waco, Texas. The sect, an offshoot of the
Seventh-Day Adventists, had been held up at
their Mount Carmel headquarters after an
armed and botched Alcohol, Tobacco, and Fire-
arms (ATF) raid, which left four government
agents and an undetermined number of Davidians dead from a brief but fierce firefight.
Throughout the fifty-one-day standoff, the government sought daily to demonize the Branch
Davidian leader, David Koresh, as a pedophile, a
false prophet, and a psychopath.

The U.S. government, its agents' egos aburst
after fifty-one days with no "progress" (i.e.,
surrender), pursued a dangerous campaign of
destruction of the front of the buildings in

preparation for "CS/tear gas insertion" and, after the thorough distribution of this airborne irritant, apparently caused a firestorm that consumed more than eighty men, women, and babies at the scene. Even before the fire had finished burning, the White House issued a statement determining suicide as the cause of death of the eighty-plus people—before a moment's investigation!

There's an old Chinese saying: "No investigation—no right to speak." And under such an adage, the White House should have been silent, at least until a full, fair, impartial investigation was conducted.

The only source suggesting the Branch Davidians killed themselves was the FBI itself, hardly an impartial source. The firestorm in Waco, Texas, which snuffed out an estimated eighty-six lives, shares eerily reminiscent precedents with the police bombing of MOVE people on May 13, 1985, in Philadelphia. Both scenes of carnage were preceded by government/media demonization campaigns that portrayed the people under government siege as insane for daring to resist the state. By contrast, the government (i.e., the police) is always seen as reasonable. In Philadelphia, where the contrasts were even sharper because of race, class, and politics, the intentional mass murder of MOVE men, women, and children was justified by the government. MOVE, they reasoned, were "terrorists"—bad niggers.

The Koreshians were "fanatics" who were suspected of physical and sexual abuse of children—thus psychologically expendable. Only after such social equations are made can the state drop bombs (as was done to MOVE) or punch holes in people's homes (as in Waco) and be reported in the media as "reasonable." Predictably, in both instances, in the hours (or minutes) following the assaults, the government justified the results as "suicide," thereby taking itself off the hook.

The initial ATF assault on Mount Carmel, purportedly for a minor weapons violation, leading up to an infernal clash of egos that launched tanks and tons of gas into the Koreshian home, was an act of colossal government arrogance and impatience. The flames and carnage of both Philadelphia and Waco merge at the strike ignited by a government that perceives itself more as a master than as a servant of the people.

April 1993

Rodney wasn't the only one

The internationally televised aggravated assault of black Los Angeles motorist Rodney King by police struck millions as a nasty revelation of the ugly underbelly of how white cops and black civilians interact in the dark streets of America. Many apologists for the police decried the King video as an aberration from the norm, and tended to justify it based on the purported threats posed by that particular "defendant" (a variation of the so-called "big nigga" defense).

At least one reputable study, however, reveals that the brutal Rodney King/LAPD encounter was just one of many across America, painting a vivid portrayal of a nationwide pattern of violent assaults by white cops against national minorities. The study, a two-year survey of both national and regional newspapers, found, in the words of study conductor Joseph Feagin, a University of Florida sociology professor, that "Rodney King's beating is not an isolated incident."

Feagin and fellow University of Florida (UF) researcher Kim Lersch utilized the NEXUS computer system to search publications from January 1990 to May 1992 to uncover 130 reports of police brutality. If one accepts the obvious, that not all such incidents are ever even reported, much less published, then it occurred at least four times a month, or once a week, during the report period. The Feagin study showed that African-Americans or Latinos were victims of the brutality in 97 percent of such cases, and white cops were centrally involved in over 93 percent of the beatings.

"We've found," said Lersch, "that the cases typically involved groups of White police officers assaulting a Black or Latino" (*In These Times*, May 3, 1993). Indeed, Lersch noted, the data revealed a national pattern that could best be termed "routine." The UF study researchers attempted to check their results against a presumably reliable source, that is, the U.S. Department of Justice.

In March 1991, when King's brutal video beating was fueling international outrage, then U.S.

attorney general Richard Thornburgh ordered a Justice Department survey for the previous six-year period. Although it was completed over a year ago, it has never been released, not even to these UF researchers.

The nationally broadcast television show *Justice Files* recently released an astonishing report revealing that in a ten-year period, from 1981 to 1991, more than *seventy-nine thousand* cases of police brutality, coast to coast, occurred. If accurate, these numbers mean more than seventy-nine hundred assaults by police a year in America. A civilian is brutalized by police, on average, more than 658 times a month, more than 164 times a week!

The police, tools of white state capitalist power, are a force creating chaos in the community, not peace. They have created more crime, more disruption, more loss of property, life, and peace than any group of criminals in the nation.

Because of the police gang in America riots are inevitable, and blame may be laid at the feet of those claiming to be "peace officers" who brutalize the people they are sworn to serve.

May 1993

L.A. outlaw

The federal trial of four Los Angeles cops, forced
by the public orgy of rebellion and rage that had
rocked the city a year before, in response to acquittals stemming from the brutal Rodney King
beating, ended in a jury compromise—two guilty,
two acquitted. Observers may be dispirited by the
fact that two cops who brutalized, traumatized,
and pummeled King were acquitted, but the trial
itself raises some serious and disturbing questions. While no one could call the writer a cop
lover, it is my firm opinion that the federal retrial
of the four L.A. cops involved in King's legalized
brutality constituted a clear violation of the Fifth
Amendment of the U.S. Constitution, which for-
bids double jeopardy. The Fifth Amendment provides, in part, that "nor shall any person be subject
for the same offense to be twice put in jeopardy of
life or limb. . . ."

For millions of African-Americans, Chicanos, and a host of Americans, the acquittals of the L.A. cop four in the Simi Valley state assault trial was an outrage that solidified the conviction that there can be no justice in the courts of this system for black people. Although not a reason for the L.A. rebellion, it certainly was a psychic straw that broke the camel's back.

The Simi Valley "trial," like the King beating itself, was both an obscenity and a commonality, for neither all-white pro-police juries nor state-sanctioned brutality are rarities to those who live in U.S. tombs as opposed to reading about them. The point is, the federal LAPD/King civil rights trial was a *political* prosecution, spurred by international embarrassment stemming from the raging flames of L.A., without which no prosecution would have occurred.

It also reveals how the system, under the pressure of an outraged people, will betray the trusts of their own agents, so one need not ask how they will treat or do treat one not their own, especially when there is public pressure to support it.

The same system that denied the four L.A. cops their alleged constitutional rights denies the rights of the poor and politically powerless

144

daily with impunity, and will further utilize the Koon case to deny others. To be silent while the state violates its own alleged constitutional law to prosecute someone we hate is but to invite silence when the state violates its own laws to prosecute the state's enemies and opponents.

This we cannot do.

We must deny the state that power.

The national ACLU is of the opinion that the second, federal prosecution violated the Fifth Amendment to the U.S. Constitution, a position that seems sound. I believe that the convictions will later be reversed on that basis by an appellate court.

It is ironic that many of those who did not oppose the federal civil prosecutions feel it inappropriate for the federal system to review state convictions under habeas corpus statutes. All this second, federal civil rights violation case has done is provide the system with camouflage, to give the appearance of justice.

The illusion is never the real.

April 1993

Absence of power

A woman working to feed the homeless gets involved in a confrontation with transit cops down in a major metropolitan subway. She is accosted, manhandled, thrown to the ground, and held under restraint. Another woman has her window shattered by highway patrol when she doesn't move her car fast enough or open her window on command. She is seized, handcuffed, and arrested.

What makes these cases remarkable is the identity of the women described here. The first, in addition to being a political leader in her own right, is the wife of a U.S. congressman. The second, a prominent professional, is the wife of a state representative. Both women are African-American.

Although the charges against these women were later dropped, the very fact that they were treated so crudely, despite their prominence and influence, makes one wonder how people without such influence are treated by agents of the state.

The two events just described occurred in Philadelphia in 1993. The first involved Philadelphia city councilwoman Mrs. Jannie Blackwell, wife of freshman U.S. representative (D) Lucian Blackwell. The second involved a leading black Philadelphia lawyer, Mrs. Renee Hughes, past president of the prestigious Barristers Association (local affiliate of the National Bar Association) and wife of state representative Vincent Hughes (D-170th District). That both cases were administratively "resolved" is of less importance than that the incidents occurred at all. Indeed, such incidents are daily occurrences in the lives of black men and women in America, regardless of class, rank, status, or station in life.

That cops can treat people so shabbily, *the very people who literally pay their salaries and set their operating budgets*, gives a grim glimmer of life at the social, economic, political bottom, where people have no influence, no clout, no voice.

These cases reveal the cold contempt white cops have for black men and women, even if

147

those women are in positions of state power and are presumed to be in control. In truth, any control is illusory, and as totally evanescent as power itself. Police are out of control. Black politicians are out of power. When these events occur, we can only conclude that if such events can happen to them, what of us?

If people can watch the massacre of MOVE people on May 13, 1985, as police firebombed MOVE headquarters, and the ATF/FBI ramming and destruction of the Koreshians of Waco, Texas, in April 1993, and still claim the police are under control, then nothing said here will convince them.

The police are agents of white ruling-class, capitalist will—period. Neither black managers nor black politicians can change that reality. The people themselves must organize for their own defense, or it won't get done.

April 1993

Clinton guillotines Guinier

Brilliant, able, scholarly, and provocative, University of Pennsylvania law professor Lani Guinier had all the necessary attributes to bring a dark luster to the foundering Clinton administration. Professor Guinier was an authentic FOB/H (Friend of Bill/Hillary) who went to Yale Law School with the "First Family," and her nomination to the post of assistant attorney general for civil rights was hailed as a bold step forward. But a concerted anti-Guinier campaign, orchestrated by a bipartisan conservative hit squad, gathered into a witch-hunt designed to destroy her chances and painted this prominent professor as a "radical," with ideas "out of the mainstream."

Faced with undercover, anonymous opposition by the Senate Judiciary Committee, fanned by attacks in the conservative press, President

149

Bill Clinton sacrificed his friend of half his life to the wolves and, in an act as startling as it was unprecedented, withdrew her nomination while denigrating her scholarship, thereby denying her the opportunity to appear before the Senate to state her case. To appease a right wing that had never supported him, Clinton gave the ax to Professor Guinier.

Clinton's withdrawal of the Guinier nomination stunned his most ardent supporters, especially African-Americans and women, who seemed hurt most by his apparent political clumsiness. This fiasco didn't occur in a vacuum but was a piece of Clinton strategy that might be termed "playing to the cheap seats." Whenever Clinton slips in the polls, his quick fix has consisted of a subtle but unmistakable appeal to the lowest common denominator in American politics—race.

When then candidate Clinton was embroiled in the Gennifer Flowers controversy, his response was a midcampaign flight to Little Rock, Arkansas, to oversee the execution of Ricky Ray Rector, a brain-damaged black man on death row. When he began to sink in the polls, his political instincts led him to denounce rapper

Sista Souljah, an affront to the Reverend Jesse Jackson, who had invited them both to speak at a Rainbow Conference.

In the first instance, he sought to divert attention from a gnawing sex scandal by demonstrating his toughness on crime. In the second, he sought to demonstrate independence from the black wing of the Democratic party. From the hiring of a Reaganite ideologue (conservative writer David Gergen) to the abandonment of Professor Guinier, the central theme was ever insult or injury to blacks, his most loyal constituency, in order to attract white so-called centrist support.

Is it mere coincidence that prior to the dumping of Guinier, Clinton's ratings were the lowest ever? The shameful sacking of Professor Guinier to appease a faction that will never accept him anyway shows that a New Democrat is no different from an Old Republican.

June 1993

Another side of *Glory*

Thanks to an old party comrade, I have had an opportunity to finally read David Hilliard's *This Side of Glory: The Autobiography of David Hilliard and the Story of the Black Panther Party* (Little, Brown, 1993). It is an interesting and tragic telling of Hilliard's life—his hardscrabble Alabaman origins, his heady elevation to chief of staff of the Black Panther Party, and his plunge into drugged defeat and dejection. It tells David's story, blemishes and all, too well. What it does not tell is the story of the Black Panther Party. In truth, there was never one party but over forty-five of them, branches and chapters with their own characters and local idiosyncrasies, scattered across the United States, with one branch in Algiers, North Africa, all united into a whole woven by a revolutionary ideal.

Because this is a review of sorts, I hereby

announce my own biases: I am a former Panther, so I offer no pretense of objectivity. I knew many of the people discussed in the book on both coasts, those living and dead, because I worked, lived in, or visited several chapters across the country as a Panther assigned to the party's Ministry of Information. I remember many beautiful and wonderful brothers and sisters who gave their all, their very lives, in defense of the party, but about them the book is largely silent. If one were to read *Glory* only, could one conclude their heroic sacrifices were, because ignored, in vain?

It tells the story of National Headquarters in Berkeley, California, or the early Oakland chapter, quite well, but by 1970 the party was a national organization, which, except for brief references to the conflicts between New York and Oakland, isn't made clear here. Each chapter reflected deep regionalisms, from California (L.A. and Oakland), which had a wealth of country southern guys and gals (Huey, David, and Geronimo were country boys, from the Deep South), to New York, where branches had Hispanic members, a faster, more up-tempo, urban pace (David even remarks on his dismay over New York "style"), to Chicago, a wicked mix of them both.

Hilliard aptly notes that Jesse Jackson borrowed from the oratory and flair of assassinated Illinois deputy chairman Fred Hampton, a masterful revolutionary organizer murdered by the government when they peeped his potential.

While Hilliard glorifies ex-prisoners who became Panthers, he largely ignores ex-Panthers who became prisoners, as well as political prisoners and POWs who have been down for decades. Hilliard is most interesting when he tells of his encounters with former Black Panther Party defense minister Dr. Huey P. Newton, an enigma worn by flesh.

Brilliant, mercurial, confident, insecure, blessed, cursed, loved, loathed—all were facets of Huey P. Newton. A self-professed homie of Huey, Hilliard doesn't examine why he, or the rest of the Peralta Street crew, couldn't pull Huey up from the pit into which he'd fallen, why none of our academia didn't utilize his brilliance at say, Howard University or Tuskegee or some other historically black college. How can a man of Huey's caliber be allowed to die in such ignominy, such squalor, such degradation?

One looks in vain for a political/radical or revolutionary perspective that survives in Hilliard's book, and in its stead one finds the author pro-moting the ten steps to sobriety from Alcoholics Anonymous rather than the socially dynamic ten-point Black Panther Party program, which still cries out for implementation almost thirty years later. People flee to drink or drugs to escape the torturous conditions that daily plague and de-value black life in this world. The very conditions that gave rise to the party in the 1960s—brutal cops, racist courts, ineffective education, jobless-ness, and the like—still plague our people to this day. A few black, largely powerless politicians pose no solutions. We still have far to go.

July 1993

What, to a prisoner, is the Fourth of July?

At a time like this, scorching irony, not convincing argument, is needed. O! Had I the ability, and could I reach the nation's ear, I would, today, pour out a fiery stream of biting ridicule, blasting reproach, withering sarcasm, and stern rebuke. For it is not light that is needed, but fire; it is not the gentle shower, but thunder. We need the storm, the whirlwind, and the earthquake. The feeling of the nation must be quickened; the conscience of the nation must be roused; the propriety of the nation must be startled; the hypocrisy of the nation must be exposed: And its crimes against God and man must be proclaimed and denounced.

What, to the American slave, is your 4th of July? I answer: a day that reveals to him, more than all the other days in the year, the gross injustice and cruelty to which he is the constant victim. To him, your celebration is a sham; your boasted liberty, an unholy license; your national greatness, swelling vanity; your sounds of rejoicing are empty and heartless; your denunciations of tyrants, brass-fronted impudence. [To the slave] your shouts of liberty and equality [are] hollow mockery; your prayers and hymns, your sermons and thanksgivings, with all your religious parade and solemnity, are, to him, mere bombast, fraud, deception, impiety and hypocrisy—a thin veil to cover up crimes which would disgrace a nation of savages. There is not a nation on the earth guilty of practices, more shocking and bloody, than are the people of these United States, at this very hour.

—Frederick Douglass, July 5, 1852

July 4, 1993, saw ANC president Dr. Nelson R. Mandela in Philadelphia quoting the Honorable Frederick Douglass's speech as he accepted the Liberty Medal, along with South African state president F. W. de Klerk. If the joint presence of Mandela and de Klerk were not enough to stir controversy, then the award presenters, Philadelphia mayor Ed Rendell and U.S. president Clinton, certainly stoked controversy among radicals. Hundreds of black Philadelphians, while certainly admirers of Dr. Mandela, took umbrage at de Klerk's presence.

Although the awarders are known as "We the People—Philadelphia," the actual everyday people of Philadelphia had little say in choosing the Liberty Medal awardees, and less say in rejecting the widely unpopular honoree de Klerk. The choice of Liberty Medalists was made not by the people but by corporate Philadelphia— big business.

Why? Why were the people, many of whom had worked for more than twenty years against apartheid (and for Mandela's release), frozen out, their protests against de Klerk all but ignored? When, or if, the African majority takes power in South Africa, U.S. big business wants friends there. If one reads the names of corporate sponsors of the award, it sounds like roll call of the Chamber of Commerce: Unisys Corp., Pennsylvania Bell, and the like.

Mandela, who has not voted in a government election in seventy-four years, and de Klerk, president by way of an election counting only minority, nonblack votes, has only the hope of liberty, no more.

The white minority in South Africa has done its level best to stifle African liberty for three hundred years.

The African majority, even after the awards, still isn't free.

July 1993

A house is not a home

She sits in utter stillness. Her coffee-brown features as if set in obsidian; as if a mask. Barely perceptible, the tears threaten to overflow that dark, proud, maternal face, a face held still by rage.

A warm spring day in North Philadelphia saw her on her way home, after her tiring duties as a housekeeper in a West Mount Airy home. On arrival, she was stopped by police, who told her she could not enter her home of twenty-three years, and that it would be torn down as part of a city program against drug dens. "My house ain't no drug den!" the fifty-nine-year-old grandmother argued. "This is my *home!*" The cops, strangers to this part of town, could care less.

Mrs. Helen Anthony left the scene, to contact her grown children. Two hours later, she returned to an eerie scene straight out of the Twilight Zone. Her home was no more.

160

A pile of bricks stood amid hills of red dust and twisted debris; a lone wall standing jagged, a man's suit flapping on a hook, flapping like a flag of surrender, after a war waged by bulldozers and ambitious politicians. Mrs. Anthony received no warning before the jaws of the baleful backhoe bit into the bricks of her life, tearing asunder the gatherings and memories of a life well lived. She was served no notice that the City of Brotherly Love intended to grind her home of twenty-three years into dust because they didn't like her neighbors; they just showed up one day, armed with television cameras and political ambitions, and did it. Gone.

When reporters asked politicos about the black grandmother whose home was demolished, they responded with characteristic arrogance: "Well, the law of eminent domain gives us the right to tear down any house we wanna," they said. When coverage turned negative, out came the olive branch:

"We'll reimburse her."

"Oops, honest mistake!"

". . . compensation. . . ."

Left unquestioned is the wisdom of a policy of mass destruction planned over a brunch of Brie and croissants executed for the six o'clock news, with no regard for the lives and well-being of the people involved.

In a city with an estimated thirty thousand homeless people, why does the government embark on a blitzkrieg of bulldozing and demolishing homes, even abandoned ones? Mrs. Anthony, offered a home in compensation by red-faced city officials, is less than enthused. "The way the city treated her," opined her daughter Geraldine Johnson, "she does not want to live in Philadelphia."

Her treatment at the hands of those who call themselves "civil servants" points to the underlying indifference with which black lives, property, and aspirations are treated by the political elite. One would be hard pressed to find this degree of destructive nonchalance in a neighborhood where a white grandmother lived.

Another chapter in the tragicomedy called "The Drug War."

April 1992

The lost generation?

Recent published reports have lamented the fact that African-American youth are remarkably resistant and virtually unresponsive to traditional, big-name public relations and big-time sports figures when they use the major media to attempt to communicate with younger blacks. The study found deep and profound alienation among youth, and a fundamental streak of fatalism about the promise of tomorrow—a sense that "tomorrow may not come, so let's live today."

The youth, while they view large blocks of TV, perceive it from the position of outsiders, knowing that the dramas, comedies, and news programs are not designed for their consumption. Only the urbo-tech musical form known as rap touches them, for it is born of urban youth consciousness and speaks to them, in their idiom, about lives lived on the margins. It is this profound disassociation that forced some nouveau middle-class blacks to lament the youth as "the lost generation."

But are they really "lost," and, if so, to whom?

The Martinican black revolutionary Frantz Fanon once opined that every generation must find its destiny and fulfill it or betray it.

In my father's generation, southern-born of the late 1890s, their destiny was to move their families north, to lands with the promise of a better life away from our hateful homelands in Dixie. The dreams of that generation, sparked by visions of new homes, better education, new cars, and prosperity, were, in relative terms, realized by some, but northbound African-Americans were never able to outrun the stigma of racism.

By the time the 1950s and 1960s generation came of age, during the Nixon-Reagan-Bush eras, race once again defined the limits of black aspirations, and with the shifting of manufacturing jobs back down south and abroad, so went dreams of relative prosperity. The children of this generation—born into sobering poverty amid shimmering opulence, their minds weaned on *Falcon Crest*ian TV excess while locked in want, watching while sinister politicians spit on their very existence—are the hip-hop/rap generation.

Locked out of the legal means of material survival, looked down upon by predatory politicians and police, left with the least relevant educational opportunities, talked at with contempt and not talked to with love—is there any question why such youth are alienated? Why the surprise?

They look at the lives they live and see not "civil rights progress" but a drumbeat of civil repression by a state at war with their dreams. Why the surprise?

This is not the lost generation. They are the children of the L.A. rebellion, the children of the MOVE bombing, the children of the Black Panthers, and the grandchildren of Malcolm; far from lost, they are probably the most aware generation since Nat Turner's; they are not so much lost as they are mislaid, discarded by this increasingly racist system that undermines their inherent worth.

They are *all* potential revolutionaries, with the historic power to transform our dull realities.

If they are lost, *find* them.

June 1992

165

Blues for Huey

The blaring trumpet of African exile Hugh Masakela screams out of the speaker, at the door of the storefront on North Philly's Columbia Avenue, soaring, plummeting, slicing a sharp, clear cut through the thick, muggy, midsummer midday mist, playing "Blues for Huey." The author sits, hypnotized by the horn, stiffened into a stupor by the Masakela sound, brassy, acute, clean, powerful, full of the melancholy sounds of tears, pain, and soggy lust crafted in dusty Soweto *shabeens*, laced with the newfound militance of black U.S. youth, Africa and Afro-America, reunited in Masakela's righteous horn, reignited into one fire.

"Blues for Huey" blared from Philadelphia's Panther office.

That awesome instrumental came, unbidden, into my consciousness when the news burst that

Huey P. Newton, the once minister of defense of the Black Panther Party, was found shot to death in an Oakland street. It hit like a Masakela solo—in the gut—in the heart! It's amazing that Huey was almost fifty; it's almost more amazing that Huey's tragedy, and ours, could be met by the innocent query of millions of black teens and preteens: "Huey who?"

I had to reach back some twenty summers to summon up "Blues for Huey," that bittersweet set that may or may not have been in homage to Newton.

Some songs mark an era, and this energetic tune does that for me.

Always a small fry in the Panther organization, I met the defense minister only once, when he came to Philadelphia and I was assigned to body-guard duties. I doubted he knew my name, but I loved him. Huey—self-taught, brilliant, taciturn, strong-willed—molded the righteous indignation and rage of an oppressed people into a national, militant, revolutionary nationalist organization. His courageous spirit touched the downtrodden, black America's so-called *lumpenproletariat* classes, and energized them into a balled fist of angry resistance, prompting FBI director J. Edgar Hoover's observation that the party posed "the most serious threat" to America's internal security. Huey woke up the historically ignored strata of black life and put them in the service of the people via free breakfast programs and free clothing programs, and organized units of community self-defense.

To the U.S. ruling class, this stirring of black life into liberational activity proved too much—enter the dogs of deception. The government unleashed the FBI, whose function, in Hoover's words, was to "frustrate every effort . . . to consolidate . . . forces or to recruit new or youthful members" by the party, which at its apex had chapters in forty-five U.S. cities.

Government efforts at disruption were swift and deadly. Setups with regional police became routine, sparked by America's historic phobia about "niggers with guns," and in the aftermath, some thirty-eight Panthers were shot down by racist cops. Party ranks were riddled with FBI-paid agents provocateurs and informants. Paranoia swelled as cop raids grew in frequency and intensity, beggaring the party through bails and legal fees.

By the mid-1970s, the party, split by government disruption and internal strife, suffering from a sharp membership decline, faded from the world's stage. Huey, a supreme commander without a command, a visionary with no outlet for his vision, a revolutionary bereft of a revolutionary party, retrogressed into the fascination of the street hustlers of his Oakland youth; the pimps, the players, the "illegitimate capitalists" (as he called them) called him. It was, to be sure, a fatal attraction.

Huey was, it must be said, no godling, no saint. He was, however, intensely human, curious, acutely brilliant, a lover of all the world's children, an implacable foe of all the world's oppressors. He rapped philosophy with the late Chinese premier Chou En-lai; he met Mao; he supped with North Korea's Kim Il Sung; he was a guest of Castro.

Huey Percy Newton, by his will and great heart, marked his age with militance, making a noble contribution to the black liberation struggle. That he could die at the hands of a crack fiend is sobering testament to how low he, and we, have fallen. The best memorial to such a one

169

is to purge our communities of the poison that plagued, and finally plugged, a truly remarkable man; and to use the highlights of his memory to spark a renewal in revolutionary consciousness.

August 1989

Philly daze:
an impressionistic memoir

If Wallace would dare to run for president in Philadelphia, we, four black North Philly teens, would dare to protest—in his white honky face, if need be. So we did, Eddie, Alvin, Dave, and I. We began by boarding the Broad Street subway and riding to the end. Four Afros amid a sea of blonds, brunettes, and redheads, entering the citadel of urban white racist sentiment to confront the Alabaman.

We must've been insane. We strolled into the stadium, four lanky dark string beans in a pot full of white, steaming limas. The band played "Dixie." We shouted, "Black power, Ungowa, black power!" They shouted, "Wallace for president! White power!" and "Send those niggers back to Africa!" We shouted, "Black power, Ungowa!" (Don't ask what "Ungowa" means. We didn't know. All we knew was that it had a helluva ring to it.) "Black power!" They hissed and booed. We stood up in our seats and proudly gave the black power salute. In answer, we received dubious gifts of spittle from those seated above. Patriots tore American flags from their standards and hurled the bare sticks at us. Wallace, wrapped in roars of approval, waxed eloquent. "When I become president, these dirty, unwashed radicals will have to move to the Sovee-yet Union! You know, all throughout this campaign these radicals have been demonstrating against George Corley Wallace. Well, I hope they have the guts to lay down in front of my car. I'll drive right over 'em!" The crowd went wild.

Helmeted cops came and told us we must leave. We protested but were escorted out (perhaps a little relieved). Outside, Eddie, Alvin, Dave, and I saw a few other blacks from Temple University and a group of young whites, also thrown out of the rally. We gathered at the bus station to get on the "C" for North Philly. But before we could board, we were attacked by several white men. One of them had a lead and leather slapjack. Outarmed and outnumbered, we fought back, but four teens were no match for eight to ten grown men.

I was grabbed by two of them, one kicking my skull while the other kicked me in the balls. Then I looked up and saw the two-toned, gold-trimmed pant leg of a Philly cop. Without thinking, and reacting from years of brainwashing, I yelled, "Help, police!" The cop saw me on the ground being beaten to a pulp, marched over briskly—and kicked me in the face. I have been thankful to that faceless cop ever since, for he kicked me straight into the Black Panther Party.

Summer in North Philly is a little like paradise to a young dude. It's so hot that sweat runs like rain in the Amazon. The air is thick with energy so real that you can smell heartbeats. The heat hangs like a haze, a loving, sticky sweet hug of Motha Nature on black flesh.

Defense captain Reg narrows his eyes in a paternal smile. "Hey, lieutenant—it's too hot to work, come on and let's get a taste." The two leave the dim Panther storefront and cross

Columbia Avenue to Webb's Bar. Johnny Webb, a man born to work with people, serves up a toothy grin and welcomes the two Panthers into his cool dark den; he wipes the glossy bartop and serves up the drinks. The captain takes a shot, and the younger Panther orders a Bitter Dog, a Philly refinement on the West Coast's Bitter Mothafucka—both composed of red wine and citrus; grapefruit in the MF, lemon in the dog. It's cool and tangy going down, and both the captain and the information lieutenant cool out in their own way. James Brown serves up southern shout from the jukebox, and Mumia screws up enough courage to ask a sister to dance. It's the Bitter Dog dancing, cause the lieutenant can't, his awkwardness causing the whole house to rock with laughter, both at his unique style (if it can be called that) and at his beat-up, scuffed-up, toes-bent-up-to-look-like-Arabian-slippers boots (which don't help much).

Jintz, a dark, lovely sister from California, laughs almost to burst. Mumia, his ears throbbin' from James Brown ("Say it loud, I'm black and I'm proud"), and wanting a breath of fresh air, sticks his head out the front door—and sees two white men dressed in army jackets kicking in the front door of the Panther office across the street. The buzz from the Bitter Dog evaporates. "Reg! Yo, Reg! Somebody breakin ina office!" The young lieutenant turns back to the street and focuses on a .38 special close enough to touch. "Freeze, nigger! If you fuckin' blink, I'll blow your black goddamn head off your shoulders!"

Red strobes sweep the summer night. Mumia freezes, and the Bitter Dog transforms itself into cold sweat. The man holding the gun smiles— sort of. His teeth are bared, but his eyes are like blue glaciers. His face and neck glow in a red flash. "This is it," the young Panther lieutenant thinks. The .38 is so close that he can smell gun oil. Across the street, white men are throwing files and papers into the street.

There I was in the 1970s, a bored, slightly petit bourgeois, burnt-out ex–Black Panther who distrusted organizations and still simmered in a stew of generational rebellion. I felt all dressed up with no place to go. The Panthers, to whom I had loaned my life, were sputtering in an inter-

necine, bicoastal, and bloody feud, East Coast
against the West Coast: those aligned with the
then minister of information Eldridge Cleaver
on the East against those siding with once minister of defense Huey P. Newton on the West.
Cleaver was an idol to me; Newton, whom I had
once served as a bodyguard, a hero. The prospect of us fighting one another sickened me. "I
didn't join the BPP to get in a goddamn gang
war!" I thought angrily to myself. "Shit! I
could've stayed in North Philly for this dumb
shit!"

The Panthers had established bona fide, sho-
nuff diplomatic relations with progressive and
revolutionary states and movements across the
globe—the People's Republic of China, North
Korea, Congo-Brazzaville, the African National
Congress, the Palestinian Liberation Organiza-
tion, Cuba, and the like. The government of
Algeria granted land for the Black Panther Party
International Section, the first embassy of the
African-American people of North America.

By 1974 the state's militia had slaughtered
more than thirty militants and jailed many more;
had seeded branch offices with informers and
agents provocateurs; had tapped phones, covered

mail, destroyed party property. Then there was an on-TV feud between Eldridge and Huey (set up by an obliging white newsman) that had resulted in two deaths. Blood for blood. East for West. Panthers croaking Panthers. I knew both men. Frustrated, angry, I drifted away from a party that had drifted away from its moorings in the people. Bitterly, I told myself that I would never join another organization. I would support, send money, write agitprop. But join? Nothin' happening. No suh! Unh unh! Not me! Then I met MOVE.

Philly, like its northern cousin New York, is a talk radio town. The pace, the political life, the sheer size of such cities makes them good breeding grounds for talk radio. Retirees, night shift workers, the unemployed, part-timers, and crackpots, all contribute to the potpourri of talk radio.

Back in the mid-1970s, a veteran announcer and all-round broadcaster named Wynn Moore began talk in Philly in a big way, virtually overnight transforming a jazz outlet into an organ for wordmongers. Tall, meaty, with piercing eyes, a pointed Vandyke, and a bass voice that rolled around the basement—that was Wynn Moore. As program director for WWDB-FM, he assembled a madcap corps of talk jocks, insurance salesmen, students, and news readers. I was one of them. He juggled us, shook us up until we fizzed, then turned us loose on the Delaware Valley. Ratings grew. Opinions flew like hatchets in a Chinese restaurant. Right-wing hosts had to abide left-wing listeners, and vice versa.

Everything that was anything and everybody that was anybody passed through DB's doors and hit the microphones. Politicians, writers, activists, sports stars, psychics, economists, and assorted loons—you name them, all were welcome on DB's airwaves. Almost all, anyway. One day I aired a brief cut from an interview with MOVE members demonstrating at the offices of the *Philadelphia Tribune*, a newspaper written for black Philadelphians. From the day I was first hired at DB I had sought audio from live sources by going to demos, news conferences, events, and incidents. Anyplace, anywhere, anytime for a sound bite: that was me. Except for world news, I never used the wires. For me, a day without audio was like a day without sunshine. And I loved sunshine (still do).

My MOVE cut was brief, and not particularly offensive, unless you happened to be an employee of the *Philadelphia Tribune*. So after the hourly newscast, I was surprised to hear a familiar voice roaring at me: "Mumia, as long as you're working here, I don't want to ever hear that MOVE shit on my radio station!" Before I could answer, Wynn turned and stalked out of the newsroom. I was shaken. I waited until the day had ended, and the red had left his face, before asking the obvious. He let out with a sigh that was half a blast of anger, and explained.

"A few years ago I was program director of a station up in Chester. Just like now, I also hosted a show. I had the bright idea to invite these MOVE nuts to my studio for an interview. It was a disaster! They took over the show—wouldn't answer a question, and I couldn't get a goddamned word in edgewise. They were ranting on, pa pa pa pa pa. They wouldn't let me moderate my own show. I couldn't speak on my own show. That was it for me. I swore then, never again." I looked at Wynn, a man I respected as brutally honest and one of the best teachers of my craft. I swallowed my own not inconsiderable pride (it was, after all, my freedom I was concerned about and not MOVE's) and followed his edict. I never aired another MOVE story while I was at his station.

Being news director of WHAT-AM meant doing the morning shift, training new talent, organizing features for the newscasts, and hosting a weekend show. I reveled in it and worked with youthful enthusiasm and energy. In 1975, the Reverend Jesse Jackson brought his show to town, and black Christian Philly erupted in a storm of support for the "country preacher."

Philadelphia PUSH (People United to Serve/ Save Humanity) hosted a national convention at the downtown Sheraton Hotel, and hundreds lined up to get in and hear Jackson. Not only would the event be broadcast live over WHAT; it would be simulcast over a network of black stations all across America. And hosting it would be—Mumia Abu-Jamal!

I was excited and eager but tried to play it off as no big thing. I worked with the engineers to get the equipment and the airtime right, and in spite of my nervousness, I knew I could handle it—and did. All went well as I interwove commentary and interviews, gospel singers and live audiences, with the words of Jesse himself. I was as high as a Georgia pine. The second day I arrived before airtime to get set up and found a small picket line in front of the Sheraton. They wore blue denim. Their hair was long, nappy, and uncombed. They were MOVE.

Delbert Africa was on the bullhorn giving Jesse hell. MOVE folks carried signs that read "THIS DUMB ASS NIGGA IS BEGGING FAVORS FROM THE SAME SYSTEM THAT OPPRESSES HIM!" Always hungry for a sound bite, I unslung my trusty tape recorder and approached Delbert. "If Jesse Jackson has gotta solution, why ain't he givin' it to everybody instead a selling it at $25 a seat? What about poor folks from North Philly, why they gotta spend they last dolla, if they got it, to hear this nigga? *John Africa* teaches us that the truth is free, like the air we breathe. It ain't to be sold." Del went on, as MOVE folks, when they get going, tend to do. I got my sound bite and more, then took the elevator up to the Jackson suite, where I found the Reverend surrounded by mostly black plainclothes cops who were working as his bodyguards.

I found him, as always, game for an interview,

181

and asked him what he thought of the demonstration out front. The Reverend looked at me like I was speaking Javanese and wrinkled his handsome features into a sneer. "I have an agenda for black people in America, young man," he said. "An A-GEN-DA! Who cares about a bunch of dirty, unwashed niggas who don't comb their hair?" Like a fool, I'd turned my Sony off. I turned it on and asked for more. This time Jesse answered, "No comment," and the police (in and out of uniform) around the room smiled.

After I heard Jesse's sincere but off-the-record sentiments, I did my broadcast from the PUSH convention that morning somewhat lacklusterly. As I left the hotel I walked back into the demo, but this time Delbert was haranguing not the air but two large black men whom I recognized from the suite upstairs. They were telling Delbert Africa to take his bullhorn and his demonstration away from the hotel. Delbert was explaining to them about freedom of speech (which is a human, not a constitutional, right for MOVE). There's plenty of freedom of speech on the next block, they said, and then they made the mistake of putting their hands on Delbert. Fists flew, a bullhorn arced, and blood spurted. Sensing news, I flicked on my Sony and dove in, dodging punches.

Within minutes the civil affairs squad was on the scene. Jesse's bodyguards were taken away to be treated for cuts and bruises, while Delbert and the other MOVE men were taken away in handcuffs. I grimaced at the obvious injustice of the whole setup, and at the apathy of the crowd that had gathered. But I had my story. That night I played it as my lead. The grunts, curses, shouts, shrieks, and yells (I always said MOVE was great sound) were the next best thing to being there.

After the broadcast my boss came into the newsroom, looking serious. I knew what he was going to say.

"Mumia, management wants to pull the tape of that demonstration and fight."

"Bernie, I can't do that. When I went to work for you, I promised to do my best to deliver the news truthfully. And you promised to back me up."

"I understand that, Mumia. But this station is cosponsoring the PUSH event. We're simulcasting across the country. We have a responsibility to see that the thing is a success."

"I agree. But let me say this. Wasn't what happened and what I aired the truth? And don't our listeners at WHAT deserve the truth?"

Bernie looked at me sideways with a half smile—a half "you smart little bastard" smile. Then a full smile broke from his lips.

"You're right, Mumia. I'll stand up to management on your side. You did a good job."

I was never prouder of that man, or of my chosen career. He could have fired me. And I thought of Jesse's haunting words: "Who cares about a bunch of dirty, unwashed niggas who don't comb their hair?"

I did.

Black radio acts as an unofficial feeder system to white radio and TV careers. It's a farm club, where talents are tested, whitenized, and then packaged for general market consumption. When I left Moore's station, I was on this track. You could hear me on the Mutual Black Network, NPR, and the Associated Press. I fancied myself an independent reporter, and I was more independent than most. I never took a story off the wires if I could write it myself.

Proud of my independence, I covered every

story, even MOVE. They were no more popular with black reporters than with white; maybe less. Their nappy-headed, aggressive, naturalistic style conflicted with the greased down, "good nigga" image the media was looking for, and most black reporters steered clear of them. I tried to be objective. Not that I went out of my way to chase them down. Not that I had to.

The change came after I read a 1975 story in the papers. It told of a night raid by cops on a MOVE gathering in West Philly. MOVE men, newly sprung from jail (they were continually in conflict with the establishment), arrived at their home early one morning. As they hugged and kissed wives and babies, a noisy, loving celebration filled the streets.

Citing neighbors' complaints, the cops came, clubs swinging. Several MOVE men were beaten, others arrested. MOVE charged brutality. The cops, of course, denied it. Standard stuff. MOVE even claimed that the cops killed a baby. Cops charged that MOVE was lying. Standard stuff. Lies from the cops. MOVE media overkill. Mumia was no green kid; I was too hip to believe either side.

MOVE called to invite me to a press conference. I refused in a friendly manner, telling their spokeswoman (Louise Africa) that I was too busy. She called me a liar. I erupted in anger. "I ain't got time for this bullshit!" "Well, make time. This ain't no game! Stop lying and tell me why you ain't coming!" I was outraged. I had never heard of a group calling a reporter a liar and abusing him for refusing to come to their press conference. As mad as a bee in a wine bottle, I hung up. And that was that. They had their press conference without Mumia.

Two days later I picked up a copy of the *Philadelphia Tribune* from a newsstand. The story was about the press conference, but a picture at the bottom of the page told the proverbial thousand words.

A black-and-white grainy photo of a light-skinned black baby boy, his tiny bruised body in a cardboard box, with fruit and yams laid beside him. I recognized him!

I must have looked at it twenty times.

Almost asleep, he looked. Peaceful in death.

I cursed myself. A few times. Quite a few times. I remembered my hot anger. I thought of my son, about Life Africa's age. I wept hot tears of shame. I cursed myself some more. Then I went back to work.

After the death of Life Africa, MOVE became more and more militant. Their confrontations with police became more frequent, their assertions of their own rights and way of life more aggressive.

On May 20, 1977, the assertion became total. MOVE men and women were seen on a wooden platform on the outside of their Powelton Village (West Philly) headquarters, armed and uniformed. Shotguns, semiautomatic weapons, dark khaki uniforms ... armed black folks! Niggas with guns!

The city went wild. Front-page photos, live video—not since the Panthers strolled the streets of Sacramento had a black organization captured the imagination of the people with simple, unapologetic militance.

"We are tired of being beaten, bones broken, and murdered babies. No longer will this system attack us with impunity. From now on, we will defend ourselves." In answer, the cops set up sniper nests around the neighborhood. Mayor (and ex-police commissioner) Frank Rizzo issued an ultimatum: "Starve 'em out!" The paramilitary option included cordoning off the neighborhood so that nothing came in or out, unless sniffed by cops. Even longstanding homeowners had to show ID to enter their own cordoned-off neighborhood. Tensions mounted. Tempers flared. But, miraculously, no shots were fired.

Meanwhile, MOVE was becoming blacker. White members, plus some Spanish and Asian members, were scared off by the police presence. Most of the blacks stood fast, even under constant surveillance, with silenced rifles pointed at them for months, angry policemen looking through the sights. The siege was one year old when MOVE agreed to allow a cop with a metal detector to sweep through the headquarters. The building was pronounced "clean."

Thus emboldened, Rizzo ordered the siege broken by armed force. On the morning of August 8, 1978, before daybreak, a shot rang out. According to then KYW reporter (now *Tribune* editor) Paul Bennet, the shot came from across the street, not from MOVE. No matter. The police hatred that had been building up for fifteen months was unleashed in a blitzkrieg of bullets. Reporters and firefighters hit the dirt.

By midday, the silence was back. One cop lay dead. Delbert Africa was beaten and pummeled, punched and kicked, into near unconsciousness. Ten MOVE people were charged with murder. I was at Rizzo's press conference. A WCAU-TV reporter, Bill Baldini, who dared to ask if any of the captives had been beaten, was tongue-lashed by the police commissioner and called a liar (even though WCAU-TV had caught it all on video). Officials lying, though, weren't news in Philly. Still aren't.

While walking to work one day, I passed in front of an idling cop car. I glanced at the driver— white, with brown hair, and wearing dark shades. He "smiled," put his hand out the car window, and pointed a finger at me, his thumb cocked back like the hammer of a gun: bang—bang— bang—the finger jerked, as if from recoil, and the cop gave it a cowboyish blast of breath before returning it to an imaginary holster. He and his pal laugh. Car rolls. Whatta joke, I thought, as I sat down to type up an interview with three women known as the Pointer Sisters, post–"salty peanuts" phase. But it was hard to concentrate. There was only one kind of pointing on my mind. And it wasn't those glitzy sisters.

On December 9, 1981, the police attempted to execute me in the street. This trial is a result of their failure to do so. Just as the police tried to kill my brothers and sisters of the family Africa on August the 8th 1978.*

I'm sleeping, sort of.

It has the languorous feel of sleep, with none of the rest. Time seems slower, easier, less oppressive. I feel strangely light. I look down and see a man slumped on the curb, his head resting on his chest, his face downcast. "Damn! That's me!" A jolt of recognition ripples through me.

A cop walks up to the man and kicks him in the face. I feel it, but don't feel it. Three cops join the dance, kicking, blackjacking the bloody, handcuffed fallen form. Two grab each arm, pull the man up, and ram him headfirst into a steel utility pole. He falls.

---

* *Commonwealth v. Abu-Jamal* 555 A.2d 846 (Pa. 1989). Mumia Abu-Jamal's statement to his jury at his sentencing hearing.

"Daddy?"

"Yes, Babygirl?"

"Why are those men beating you like that?"

"It's okay, Babygirl, I'm okay."

"But why, Daddy? Why did they shoot you and why are they hitting and kicking you, Abu?"

"They've been wanting to do this for a long time, Babygirl, but don't worry, Daddy's fine— see? I don't even feel it!"

The chubby-cheeked child's face softly melts into the features of a broad-nosed, bald, gold-toothed, and grizzled old man, his dark brown skin leathery and nicely wrinkled.

"Boy, you all right?"

"Yeah, Dad, I'm okay."

"I love you, boy."

"And I love you, Daddy."

The "I love you" echoes like feedback, boom-ing like a thousand voices, and faces join the calming cacophony: wife, mother, children, old faces from down south, older faces from— Africa? Faces, loving, warm, and dark, rushing, racing, roaring past. Consciousness returns to find me cuffed, my breath sweet with the heavy metallic taste of blood, in darkness.

I lie on the paddy wagon floor and am informed by the anonymous crackle on the radio that I am en route to the police administration building a few blocks away.

I feel no pain—just the omnipresent pressure that makes every bloody breath a labor.

I recall my father's old face with wonder at its clarity, considering his death twenty years before.

I am en route to the Police Administration Building, presumably on the way to die.

Afterword

The trial of
Mumia Abu-Jamal

Leonard I. Weinglass
Attorney for Mumia Abu-Jamal

In one of the most extraordinary trials in recent history, Mumia Abu-Jamal, a leading African-American broadcast journalist in Philadelphia, aptly dubbed, "the voice of the voiceless," was put on trial in June 1982 and sentenced to death for the murder of a white police officer. The case was tried before the Honorable Albert Sabo, notorious for having put more people on death row than any other sitting judge in the United States. Before ascending to the bench, he served as the undersheriff in Philadelphia for sixteen years. No less distinguished was the tough and experienced prosecutor who had previously obtained the murder conviction of an innocent man.*

---

* *Commonwealth v. Connor*

After the defendant in that case had served twelve years for a crime he didn't commit, the district attorney's office successfully petitioned the court for his release based on evidence that indicated that the defendant had not committed the crime, and following an investigation into the original trial evidence and testimony.

The only inexperienced actor in Mumia's case was the court-appointed attorney, who was thrust into the role of defense counsel after Mumia was stripped of his right to represent himself midway through jury selection. The attorney repeatedly sought to be relieved as assisting counsel to Mumia during pretrial hearings.

It would have been impossible for counsel to defend Mumia effectively no matter what his skill and dedication. The court allocated only $150 pretrial to the defense for the investigation of the case despite the fact that the police investigators had conducted more than 125 witness interviews. By trial time, the defense had succeeded in locating just two eyewitnesses, although aware that there were many more. In a desperate last-minute move, Mumia's attorney frantically tried to convince a key eyewitness to come to court by calling on the judge's telephone while the jury sat waiting in the courtroom. The effort failed. While the prosecution presented experts on ballistics and pathology, the defense was prevented from doing so due to the paltry sums allocated by the court for that purpose.

On the third day of jury selection, the court barred Mumia from further questioning of prospective jurors. Reluctantly, and obviously unprepared, his court-appointed attorney was compelled to take over. Although seventy-seven of the first eighty jurors had heard or read of the case, necessitating a probing inquiry into what opinions, if any, they had formed, the court became impatient with the process, claiming that Mumia's questions intimidated jurors. Some court observers believed that the court's action might more plausibly be attributed to the fact that Mumia's professional training in broadcast journalism was creating too favorable an impression.

Under pressure from the court to expedite the selection process, which at one point included threatening Mumia's lawyer with contempt, a jury was selected that included a man whose best friend was a former Philadelphia police officer on disability after being shot while on duty, as well as an alternate juror whose husband was a Philadelphia police officer. Counsel inexplicably failed to object or even make note of the prosecution's racially skewed use of eleven of fifteen peremptory challenges to remove African-American jurors. He even consented to the judge's summary dismissal, in Mumia's absence, of an African-American juror who had already been selected, replacing her with an older white male, who refused to answer whether he could keep an open mind, saying he didn't think he "could be fair to both sides."

The prosecution presented its case in less than seven days. Mumia was not present during most of it, having been removed from the courtroom for insisting on his right to self-representation, as well as the assistance of *John Africa* at counsel table. With his life on the line, he argued that he was being defended by a lawyer who was not only unqualified but unwilling to represent him. Nothing was done to assist Mumia in following the proceedings, such as transmission into his holding cell or the provision of a transcript. Not only was this a departure from common practice, but it was particularly damaging since it was Mumia, and not his attorney, who had prepared

the case. Without Mumia's presence or assistance, his attorney could only feebly attempt to
cross-examine the prosecution's witnesses.

That the police officer had been shot on a
public street at 4 A.M. on December 9, 1981,
after having stopped Mumia's brother's car was
undisputed. That Mumia arrived at the scene
moments after the officer had pummeled his
brother with his flashlight was also undisputed.
Mumia was shot, presumably by the same officer,
since the bullet taken from his body matched
that of the officer's gun. Mumia remained in
critical condition for a period of time following
emergency surgery. Nonetheless, his case was
rushed to trial within six months without a con-
tinuance. After announcing that he would defend himself, Mumia was given just three weeks
to prepare his case for trial.

The prosecution's case relied mainly on the
testimony of four witnesses who claimed to be at
or near the scene of the shootings. The court had
refused all requests to have these witnesses attempt an identification of Mumia in a lineup,
instead allowing him to be identified as he sat
at counsel table or through photographs in
his absence. The most damaging witness was

a female prostitute who had a record of over thirty-five arrests and was serving a sentence in Massachusetts. She testified that she saw Mumia shoot the officer by running up behind him, shooting him once, and then firing again after he fell to the sidewalk. Previously, she had given a number of differing accounts, most of them contradicted by the other three witnesses. Another prostitute who was working the same area that night testified she was offered the same deal as the prosecution's witness: immunity from arrest by the police in return for her testimony against Mumia.

Of the three remaining witnesses, all male, two said they saw Mumia run to the scene where the police officer was beating Mumia's brother. Both testified that gunfire erupted shortly after Mumia arrived, but neither one saw Mumia shoot the officer. The third witness, a cabdriver who had pulled up behind the police car, was closest to the shooting. He told police that the shooter fled the scene, before more police arrived, by running to where an alleyway intersects the sidewalk some thirty yards away. The shooter was a large, heavy man, over six feet two and weighing more than 225 pounds. Mumia is six feet one and weighed a scant 170 pounds. At trial this witness denied that the shooter ran away, insisting instead that he took just a few steps and then sat down on the curb at the precise point where the police found Mumia, slumped over and bleeding profusely from his wound. The judge kept from the jury the fact that this witness had previously been convicted of throwing a Molotov cocktail into a public school for pay and was then on parole. He might have altered his testimony to curry favor with the prosecution or even out of fear. Another witness, a nearby resident, also reported seeing a man flee the scene in the same direction. She was the witness that defense counsel couldn't produce after contacting her on the judge's telephone midway through trial. A third witness, a prostitute, told the authorities that she also observed one or two men running from the scene, but recanted her story after lengthy questioning by the police. In all, four witnesses situated in four separate locations on the street—none of whom knew each other or Mumia—reported seeing the shooter flee, and all had him going in precisely the same direction. It's simply impossible that all four were hallucinating about the very same thing. Nonetheless, no investigation was made to locate or identify the fleeing suspect.

The prosecution's theory was that Mumia first shot the officer, wounding him slightly. When the officer returned fire and hit him, Mumia, angered, stood over the officer, who had since fallen to the sidewalk, and shot him in the face, killing him instantly. None of the witnesses, however, saw it that way. None even saw Mumia get shot. That theory was constructed out of the simple fact that the police found both Mumia and the officer lying within several feet of each other on the sidewalk, both wounded from gunshots. Although Mumia's gun was found at the scene (he had a permit to carry a weapon because he had been robbed as a cabdriver), the prosecution's expert claimed he could not match the bullet recovered from the officer's body to Mumia's gun due to the fragmented nature of the bullet.

To add weight to its somewhat shaky thesis, unconfirmed by the incredible prosecution witnesses, the prosecution produced a security guard who worked at the hospital where Mumia was taken for treatment. She testified that

Mumia, an experienced journalist who had covered scores of court cases, openly confessed to everyone within earshot that he had shot the policeman, adding for emphasis, "I hope the motherfucker dies." But the officer who took Mumia into custody and stayed with him stated in his written report that Mumia remained silent throughout the entire time he was with him. His testimony, however, like that of the missing eyewitnesses, was not produced at trial. The officer who reported these events was "on vacation" when he should have been available to be called by the defense. A defense request to continue the case a few days until his return was denied.

Not able to produce the witnesses it needed to rebut the prosecution's case, the defense relied instead on the testimony of sixteen character witnesses. All testified that Mumia could not possibly have committed such a crime because he was known both professionally and socially as a gentle and decent man. When one character witness, the noted author and poet Sonia Sanchez, took the stand, the prosecutor questioned her, over objection, about the irrelevant fact that she had written the foreword to Assata Shakur's (Joanne Chesimard's) book, *Assata Speaks*. Then, with the court's blessing, he launched into a highly prejudicial and improper line of questioning about Assata's conviction for killing two police officers in New Jersey; inquiring, further, whether Sanchez also politically supported three New York men who had been convicted of killing police. Thus the prosecutor insinuated that Sanchez made a habit of supporting police killers, and that, by implication, Mumia must be one. In so doing, the prosecutor not only committed prosecutorial misconduct but set the stage for what later became an all-out attack on Mumia's politics.

The jury began deliberations at noon on the Friday of the Fourth of July weekend. By then they had been sequestered in a downtown hotel and away from their families for almost three weeks. Not surprisingly, before the day was over they had reached a verdict—guilty of first-degree murder. However, they were unable to do so without first requesting, following several hours of deliberation, that they be reinstructed on the law of third-degree murder and manslaughter. Evidently, at least some jurors were troubled by the fact that, even if they accepted the prosecution's theory of the case, the element of premeditation was lacking because the officer was not shot fatally until after Mumia himself was shot; and then, presumably, as the result of an unpremeditated reaction. With the jury thus conflicted on the lesser charges of manslaughter and third-degree murder, no one anticipated this same jury would vote the death penalty.

The key to understanding why they did lies in what transpired during that part of the case that followed, referred to as the penalty phase. It is then that both sides present evidence bearing on the issue of whether a sentence of life without parole or a sentence of death should be imposed. In a clear violation of Mumia's constitutional rights, the prosecution presented evidence of Mumia's background as a member of the Black Panther Party some twelve years earlier and his political beliefs as reported in a newspaper interview when he was just sixteen years old. Beyond doubt Mumia is on death row because of those political beliefs and associations. The ensuing portion of the transcript reads like a grotesque chapter out of the Inquisition.

It began when Mumia rose at counsel table to read a statement to the jury, exercising the time-honored right of allocution that all convicted

205

persons have prior to being sentenced. He was not sworn as a witness and did not take the stand. In his statement he expressed his innocence and eloquently claimed that the proceedings were unfair. Stunned by Mumia's accusations against his handling of the case, the judge ruled that Mumia had made himself a witness and could be cross-examined in front of the jury. The prosecutor only too eagerly rose to the occasion.

First, Mumia was asked why he didn't stand for the judge when he entered the courtroom. That irrelevant and prejudicial inquiry was followed in rapid succession by a series of questions about why Mumia didn't accept the court's rulings without rancor, shouted at an appellate judge when his right to control his own case was taken away, and engaged in a hostile exchange with the court during pretrial hearings. As if to answer these questions, the prosecutor read from a twelve-year-old newspaper article about the Black Panther Party that contained, among other things, an interview of Mumia when he was just sixteen years old.* With his voice rising, the prosecutor demanded to know whether

* *Philadelphia Inquirer*, January 4, 1970.

Mumia had ever said that "political power grows
out of the barrel of a gun." Mumia calmly responded that the quote did not originate with
him but was a well-known dictum of Chairman
Mao Ze-dong of the People's Republic of China.
Continuing without letup, the prosecutor asked
if Mumia could recall having said, in the same
interview, "All power to the people." Again
Mumia acknowledged the quote but insisted on
the right to read extensively from the news article in order to place his comments in context.
The article, which had previously been kept out
of evidence by the court for being too prejudicial, included references to the Black Panther
Party, the breakfast program, and the party's on-
going dispute with the Philadelphia Police Department.

Having thus portrayed Mumia as a radical
black militant to this nearly all-white jury, the
prosecutor argued in summation that it was
Mumia's political history and disrespect of the
system that caused him to kill the policeman.
The jury returned a verdict of death, after being
allowed to focus on the irrelevant quoted words
of a sixteen-year-old, and disregarding the fact
that Mumia had grown into manhood without a

207

single conviction on his record, had a family, and the abiding respect and admiration of the community.

The appeal that followed was no less irregular. A year passed before Judge Sabo got around to formally pronouncing the sentence of death. Mumia's first assigned appellate attorney did nothing for an additional year and had to be removed from the case by the appellate court. His replacement counsel required another year to reconstruct events and file the necessary papers. Part of that reconstruction was an affidavit from Mumia's trial attorney testifying to the number of African-Americans who had been removed from the jury. Due to the passage of time, the Pennsylvania Supreme Court disregarded the affidavit, alleging that the attorney's memory had faded in the interim. All relief was denied. Only four justices, the minimum number required, signed the court's opinion.* One of the four, Justice McDermott, clearly should have disqualified himself, because he had been involved in a direct and personal court confronta-

---

* *Commonwealth v. Abu-Jamal* 521 Pa. 188, 555 A.2d 846 (1989).

tion with Mumia, but didn't. Chief Justice Nix, an African-American, inexplicably removed himself from the case, as did another justice, Justice Larson, also without comment. That justice had been accused of racial bias by the chief and was later prosecuted for a minor drug offense, convicted, and subsequently removed from the bench following impeachment by the Pennsylvania Senate.

The court's opinion, a particularly vituperative fifteen-page document, possibly the result of Justice McDermott's personal encounter with Mumia, rejected all of Mumia's claims respecting constitutional and trial errors. Sanctioned was the prosecutor's racially skewed use of peremptory challenges, the court's deprivation of Mumia's right to defend himself and be present, and the improper cross-examination of both Sonia Sanchez and Mumia. Most remarkably, the prosecutor's argument to the jury that Mumia would have "appeal after appeal and perhaps there could be a reversal of the case, or whatever, so that may not be final," was upheld. That precise argument, undermining the need of the jury to confront the finality of what they were being asked to do, was specifically rejected by the U.S. Supreme Court in 1985.* Earlier the Pennsylvania Supreme Court had reversed a state conviction that, ironically, was based on a summation given by the very same prosecutor using the nearly identical argument he made in Mumia's case.† The court chose to ignore both these precedents and affirmed Mumia's death sentence.

Mumia fared no better with the U.S. Supreme Court. It refused to even consider his appeal.‡ However, that same year it accepted, and decided favorably, a case in which a member of the Aryan Brotherhood, a white racist organization, complained that the prosecution had improperly used the fact of his political association against him in the penalty phase of his trial. Ruling that the First Amendment to the Constitution bars such evidence, the Court reversed his death sentence.§ Mumia's petition to be joined in this appeal was denied without comment.

Now, more than twelve years after his conviction, Mumia is seeking a new trial in the state

---

* *Caldwell v. Mississippi* 472 U.S. 320 (1985).

† *Commonwealth v. Baker* 511 Pa. 1, 511 A.2d 777 (1986).

‡ *Pennsylvania v. Abu-Jamal* 498 U.S. 881 (1990).

§ *Dawson v. Delaware* 503 U.S. 159 (1992).

courts of Pennsylvania. If denied, he plans to file a habeas corpus petition in the federal courts. However, new restrictions imposed by the U.S. Supreme Court on habeas corpus severely restrict his ability to obtain any relief.

For the first time, his case is being investigated. Evidence has already been found in support of his innocence. However, investigating his case more than a decade after the event has proven both difficult and expensive.

At the time of this writing, a death warrant has not yet been signed by the governor. But because of the November 1994 election of Republican governor Thomas Ridge who ran, in part, on expediting executions, there is danger that in early 1995 an execution date will be set. Mumia is near the top of the list of those awaiting the signing of a warrant, so we are in a race against time to save this innocent and, as the preceding pages attest, eloquent "voice of the voiceless." In the words of Ossie Davis, cochair of the Committee to Save Mumia Abu-Jamal, "We need Mumia desperately. At a time like this, we cannot afford to let them take such a voice from us without putting up a fight of enormous proportions."

About the Author

Mumia Abu-Jamal was born April 24, 1954, in Philadelphia.

At the time of his arrest on December 9, 1981, on charges of murder of Philadelphia police officer Daniel Faulkner, Mumia Abu-Jamal was a well-known Philadelphia-based African-American journalist and activist. He was the president of the Philadelphia chapter of the Association of Black Journalists. The January 1981 issue of *Philadelphia* magazine had named him "one of the people to watch in 1981."

During the period of 1970–1981 he was a widely acclaimed and Corporation for Public Broadcasting award-winning journalist, known as "the voice of the voiceless" as a result of his news broadcasts on National Public Radio, Mutual Black Network, and National Black Network, and did daily reports on WUHY (now WHYY) and a number of other stations.

From his youth, Mumia was a political activist. At age fourteen, he was beaten and arrested for protesting a presidential rally for George Wallace. In the fall of 1968, he became a founding member and Lieutenant minister of information of the Philadelphia chapter of the Black Panther Party. During the summer of 1970, Mumia worked at the Black Panther Party newspaper in Oakland, California, returning to Philadelphia shortly before the Philadelphia police raid on all three offices of the Black Panther Party.

While working as a journalist during the 1970s, Mumia published some hard-hitting criticism of the Philadelphia Police Department and the Rizzo administration, which also made him a man for them "to watch." He rejected Rizzo's version of the 1978 siege of the MOVE organization's Powelton Village home by more than six hundred heavily armed officers, and his tireless advocacy resulted in his being fired from his broadcast job. He had to work as a night-shift cabdriver to support his family.

He was driving a cab the night of December 9, 1981, when he was shot and beaten by police and charged with the murder of a police officer. He was put on trial within six months, and on July 3, 1982, he was convicted of murder and sentenced to death. His appeal to the Pennsylvania Supreme Court was denied in March 1989, and the U.S. Supreme Court has refused review of his case. A petition for postconviction relief is now being prepared for filing in the state courts.

For thirteen years he has been on death row in Huntingdon prison. He has been a working journalist from death row for over five years—his commentaries have been printed in dozens of newspapers (at least forty are known) throughout the United States and Europe. In January 1991 his commentary on life on death row and the impact of the *McCleskey* case was featured in the *Yale Law Journal*.

In 1994 his scheduled commentaries for National Public Radio's *All Things Considered*, "Live from Death Row," which described life behind bars in Huntingdon, caused such controversy that they were abruptly canceled, sparking intense debates across the country about censorship and the death penalty.

For more information on racism, the death penalty, and what you can do, contact

International Concerned Friends & Family of Mumia Abu-Jamal
P.O. Box 19709
Philadelphia, PA 19143
215-476-8812 phone & fax

Equal Justice USA, A Project of the Quixote Center
P.O. Box 5206
Hyattsville, MD 20782
301-699-0042 phone
301-864-2182 fax

Free Mumia Abu-Jamal Coalition
P.O. 650
New York, NY 10009
212-330-8029

Committee to Save Mumia Abu-Jamal
163 Amsterdam Ave. #115
New York, NY 10023-5001
212-580-1022

Partisan Defense Committee
P.O. Box 99
Canal St. Station
New York, NY 10013
212-406-4252

Western PA Committee to Free Mumia
Abu-Jamal
P.O. Box 10174
Pittsburgh, PA 15232-0174

Art & Writings Against Death Penalty
164 Lexington Ave.
Jersey City, NJ 07304
201-435-3244

Freedom Now Network!
2420 24th St.
San Francisco, CA 94110
415-648-4505

Just Justice
c/o Claude Pujol, UFR d'anglais, 3
Rue des Tanneurs, 37041
Tours Cedex France
33-47-61-69-37 phone

Refuse & Resist!
305 Madison Ave., Suite 1166
New York, NY 10165
212-713-5657